W9-APM-239

STEM Labs for Earth & Space Science

MARION COUNTY PUBLIC
LIBRARY SYSTEM
321 Monroe Street
Fairmont, WV 26554
(304) 366-1210

Grades 6–8

Authors: Schyrlet Cameron and Carolyn Craig
Editor: Mary Dieterich
Proofreaders: Cindy Neisen and Margaret Brown

COPYRIGHT © 2017 Mark Twain Media, Inc.

ISBN 978-1-62223-639-8

Printing No. CD-404260

Mark Twain Media, Inc., Publishers
Distributed by Carson-Dellosa Publishing LLC

MAR 2 9 20

Table of Contents

To the Teacher

STEM is an acronym for **Science, Technology, Engineering,** and **Mathematics**. STEM education is an initiative designed to get students interested in these career fields. STEM learning emphasizes students gaining knowledge and developing skills needed for a twenty-first-century workforce.

STEM Labs is a three-book series. The books in the series include *STEM Labs for Life Science, STEM Labs for Physical Science,* and *STEM Labs for Earth & Space Science.* The series provides fun and meaningful integrated activities designed to cultivate student interest in topics of the STEM fields. All the activities in the series are lab investigations that support the national standards: Next Generation Science Standards (NGSS) developed by the National Teachers of Science Association (NTSA), National Council of Teachers of Mathematics Standards (NCTM), Standards for Technology Literacy (ITEA), and Common Core State Standards (CCSS). Each book includes:

- **Instructional Resources:** A set of informational handouts to guide students in successfully completing STEM investigations.
- **Lab Challenges:** Investigations promoting the STEM fields (science, technology, engineering, and mathematics). Labs emphasize designing an object, process, model, or system to solve a problem.
- **Rubrics:** Scoring guides to explain the set of criteria used for assessing the projects.

STEM Labs for Earth & Space Science contains 26 lab activities that challenge students to apply scientific inquiry, content knowledge, and technological design to solve a real-world problem. Key components of every lab activity are creativity, teamwork, communication, and critical thinking. Each lab activity requires students to:

- **Research:** Students find out what is already known about the topic being investigated.
- **Collaborate:** Students complete activities in collaborative groups. They are encouraged to communicate openly, support each other, and respect contributions of members as they pool perspectives and experiences toward solving a problem.
- **Design:** Students use creativity and imagination to design an object, process, model, or system. Students test the design, record data, and analyze and interpret results.
- **Reflect:** Students think back on the process in a way that further promotes higher-order thinking.

STEM Labs for Earth & Space Science is written for classroom teachers, parents, and students. This book can be used to supplement existing curriculum or enhance after-school or summer-school programs.

Introduction to STEM

STEM Education

The STEMs of Learning: **Science**, **Technology**, **Engineering**, and **Mathematics** is an initiative designed to get students interested in these career fields. In 2009, the National Academy of Engineering (NAE) and the National Research Council (NRC) reported that there was a lack of focus on the science, technology, engineering, and mathematics (STEM) subjects in K–12 schools. This creates concerns about the competitiveness of the United States in the global market and the development of a workforce with the knowledge and skills needed to address technical and technological issues.

STEM Education	
STEM	**Knowledge and Skills Needed to Address Technical and Technological Issues**
Science	**Basic science process skills** include the basic skills of classifying, observing, measuring, inferring, communicating, predicting, manipulating materials, replicating, using numbers, developing vocabulary, questioning, and using cues. **Integrated science skills** (more complex skills) include creating models, formulating a hypothesis, generalizing, identifying and controlling variables, defining operationally, recording and interpreting data, making decisions, and experimenting.
Technology	**Design process** includes identifying and collecting information about everyday problems that can be solved by technology. It also includes generating ideas and requirements for solving the problems.
Engineering	**Design process** includes identifying a problem or design opportunity; proposing designs and possible solutions; implementing the solution; evaluating the solution and its consequences; and communicating the problem, processes, and solution.
Mathematics	**Mathematical skills** include the ability to use problem-solving skills, formulate problems, develop and apply a variety of strategies to solve problems, verify and interpret results, and generalize solutions and strategies to new problems. Students also need to be able to communicate with models, orally, in writing, and with pictures and graphs; reflect and clarify their own thinking; use the skills of reading, listening, and observing to interpret and evaluate ideas; and be able to make conjectures and convincing arguments.

Characteristics of a STEM Lesson

STEM education emphasizes a new way of teaching and learning that focuses on hands-on inquiry and open-ended exploration. It allows students with diverse interests, abilities, and experiences to develop skills they will need in the 21st-century workforce. It is a shift away from the teacher presenting information and covering science topics to the teacher guiding and assisting students in problem solving while encouraging them to take the lead in their own learning.

Characteristics of a STEM Lesson

- Stimulates the curiosity and interest of both girls and boys
- Emphasizes hands-on, inquiry-based learning
- Addresses both math and science standards
- Encourages the use of and/or creation of technology
- Involves the engineering design process
- Stresses collaborative teamwork

10 Steps in a STEM Lesson

Students are presented with a challenge to design a model, process, or system to solve a problem. They work on the challenge in collaborative teams of three or four students, depending on the STEM lesson. Each team follows a set of problem-solving steps in order to find a solution.

Step #1:   Research the problem and solutions.
Step #2:   Brainstorm ideas about how to design a model, process, or system to solve the problem.
Step #3:   Draw a diagram of the model, process, or system.
Step #4:   Construct a prototype.
Step #5:   Test the prototype.
Step #6:   Evaluate the performance of the prototype.
Step #7:   Identify how to improve the design of the prototype.
Step #8:   Make the needed changes to the prototype.
Step #9:   Retest and reevaluate the prototype.
Step #10: Share the results.

Introduction to STEM

Collaborative Learning Teams

Collaborative learning is a successful teaching strategy in which small groups of students, each with different levels of ability and diverse interests and experiences, work together to solve a problem, complete a task, or create a product. The responsibility for learning is placed squarely on the shoulders of the students. Each student is individually accountable for their own work, and the work of the group as a whole is also evaluated. The role of the teacher is to guide and assist the students in the problem-solving process. A collaborative learning environment in the science classroom has many benefits.

Benefits of Collaborative Learning

- Engages students in active learning
- Encourages students to communicate openly
- Motivates students to cooperate and support each other
- Teaches respect for contributions of all members
- Prepares students for the real world

Team Dynamics

It is important that the teacher organizes the classroom into teams. Teams should consist of three or four students, depending on the STEM activity. Fewer members may limit the diversity of ideas, skills, and approaches to problem solving.

Assigning Roles

A successful collaborative learning experience requires a division of the workload among the members of a team. The teacher may wish to assign the role of each member of the team as follows:

- **Team Captain** is responsible for keeping the group on-task.

- **Recorder** is responsible for organizing the paperwork and creating drawings, diagrams, or illustrations as needed.

- **Materials Manager** is responsible for gathering the needed materials and supplies for the project.

- **Monitor** is responsible for keeping the work area tidy and for properly storing the project at the end of the class.

STEM: Preparing Students for the 21st Century

Recent shifts in education are being driven by colleges and businesses demanding that high school graduates have the "21st-century skills" necessary for success in today's world. They are advocating schools teach students certain core competencies such as collaboration, critical thinking, and problem solving. STEM education focuses on these skills and, at the same time, fosters student interests in the fields of science, technology, engineering, and mathematics.

Why STEM Education?

STEM Promotes:
- student-centered learning.
- collaboration and teamwork.
- equality (equally benefits boys and girls).
- critical-thinking skills.
- hands-on, inquiry-based learning.
- use of technology.
- engineering design process.
- opportunities to apply math skills and knowledge.
- greater depth of subject exploration.
- innovation.
- real-world problem solving.
- curiosity and creativity.
- teachers as facilitators and monitors of learning.

Common Hurdles to STEM Education

STEM Requires:
- students have baseline skills in reading, math, and science to be successful.
- students be able to work well with others.
- flexible lesson plans; projects may take one class period to several weeks to complete.

The Pieces of STEM

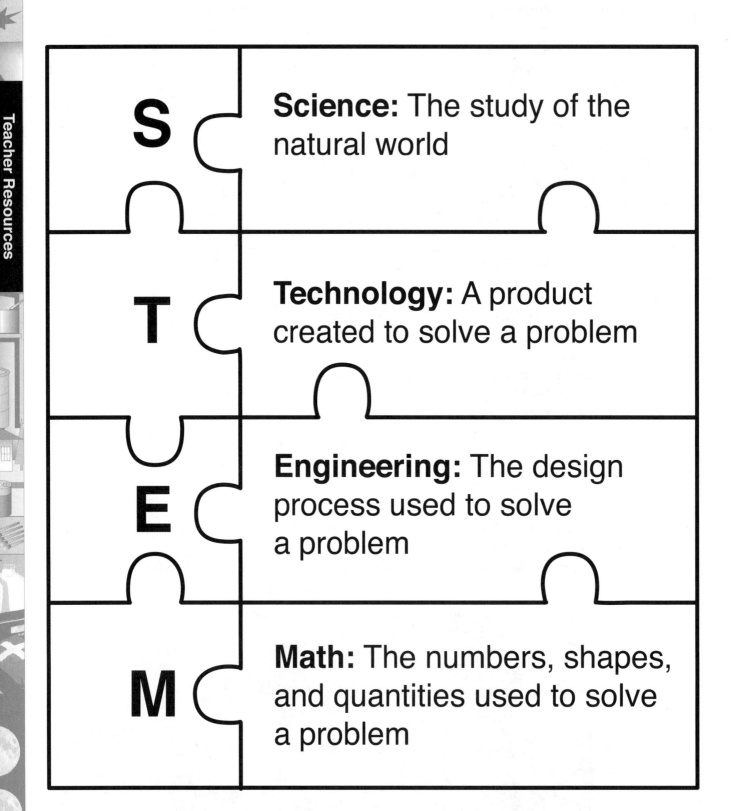

Science: The study of the natural world

Technology: A product created to solve a problem

Engineering: The design process used to solve a problem

Math: The numbers, shapes, and quantities used to solve a problem

10 Tips for Student Collaboration

1. Respect Each Other and All Ideas

2. No "Put Downs"

3. Be a Good, Active Listener

4. Come Well Prepared for Task Assignment

5. Participate and Contribute During Discussions

6. Support Your Opinions

7. Promote Positive Team-Member Relations

8. Disagree in an Agreeable Manner

9. Encourage Team Members

10. Complete Assignment on Time and With Quality Work

Name: _____

Date: _____

STEM Lab Challenge Rubric

Task	4	3	2	1
Research	Demonstrates planned technological and other research/inquiry that leads to educated decisions; all information cited following copyright guidelines	Demonstrates technological and other research/inquiry; most information cited	Demonstrates some technological and other research/inquiry; some information cited	Demonstrates no technological and other research/inquiry; no information cited
Model Process or System	Drawing has labels and advanced explanation of strategy	Drawing has labels and explanation of strategy	Drawing has some labels and partial explanation of strategy	Drawing has no labels or explanation of strategy
Results	All records, analysis, and interpretation of test results in organized, accurate manner	Records, analysis, and interpretation of test results completed	Records, analysis, and/ or interpretation of test results incomplete	No records, analysis, or interpretation of test results
Conclusion	Demonstrates high-level thinking when summarizing the purpose, test procedure, and test results	Demonstrates thinking skills summarizing the purpose, test procedure, and test results	Demonstrates some thinking skills summarizing the purpose, test procedure, and test results	Demonstrates no thinking skills summarizing the purpose, test procedure, and test results
Reflection	Reflection completed with thoughtful insight into team's choices	Reflection completed with insight into team's choices	Reflection partially completed with little insight into team's choices	Reflection incomplete
Evaluation	Self-evaluation completed with thoughtful insights about behavior and performance as a team member	Self-evaluation completed with insights	Self-evaluation partially completed; some insights	Self-evaluation incomplete—no insights

Teacher Comments:

Name: _____   Date: _____

STEM Lab Self-Evaluation Rubric

Directions: Circle the description in each category that you believe best describes your behavior and performance during the assigned lab challenge.

Category	4	3	2	1
Attitude	Always positive attitude about the challenge; never critical of the project or the work of other team members	Mostly positive attitude about the challenge; rarely critical of the project or the work of other team members	Usually positive attitude about the challenge; sometimes critical of the project or the work of other team members	Negative attitude about the challenge; often critical of the project or the work of other team members
Work Quality	Highest quality work	High quality work	Work occasionally needs to be redone by others to ensure quality	Work needs to be redone by others to ensure quality
Innovative Problem Solving	Seeks multiple, innovative solutions to the problem to meet the challenge	Seeks some innovative solutions to the problem to meet the challenge	Seeks a few possible solutions to the problem to meet the challenge	Seeks no solutions to the problem to meet the challenge
Contributions	Consistently works to fulfill challenge requirements and perform individual team-member role	Frequently works to fulfill challenge requirements and perform individual team-member role	Sometimes works to fulfill challenge requirements and perform individual team-member role	Seldom works to fulfill challenge requirements and perform individual team-member role
Lab Focus	Focuses with team members to complete the lab challenge without having to be reminded; self-directed	Focuses with team members to complete the lab challenge; rarely needs reminding; reliable team member	Sometimes focuses with team members to complete the lab challenge; often needs reminding; unreliable team member	Seldom focuses with team members to complete the lab challenge; often disruptive; unreliable team member

Student Comments:

Reflection

Name: _____ Date: _____

Title of Lab Challenge: _____

Directions: Complete the following statements about your lab challenge.

One thing I didn't expect from this challenge was	If I want to get better at scientific investigation, I need to
One thing I would improve if I did this lab again would be	One thing I would like to learn more about after doing this investigation is
After completing this challenge, I realize that	The hardest part of this investigation was

From completing this investigative lab, I now understand

Rock and Mineral Identification Kit: Teacher Information

STEM Lab Overview

Students are challenged to design a kit that can be used to perform a variety of physical property tests on rocks and minerals in the field or the classroom. The kit should include samples of common rocks and minerals and a detailed instruction manual.

Concepts

- Crystal • Mineral • Rock • Rock cycle

Standards for Grades 6–8

NGSS	NCTM	ITEA	CCSS
-Earth's Systems	-Problem Solving -Communication -Connections -Representation	-Nature of Technology -Technology and Society -Technological World	-English Language Arts Standards: Science & Technical Subjects

Teaching Strategies

Step #1: Engage—Review concepts. Introduce the STEM lab. Discuss the challenge presented in the lab, providing students with an opportunity to connect previous knowledge to the problem they are to solve.

Step #2: Investigate—Students conduct research to gain an understanding of the major science concepts related to the topic, review possible solutions to the lab challenge, and formulate new ideas for solving the problem.

Step #3: Explore—Students apply research to design and test a model, process, or system to solve the problem presented in the challenge.

Step #4: Communicate—Students share results.

Step #5: Evaluate—Students are given an opportunity to reflect on what they have learned.

Managing the Lab

- Set a deadline for project submission and presentations.
- Group students into collaborative teams and assign roles.
- Review prerequisite skills students need for doing the lab, such as measuring, weighing, constructing, recording data, graphing, and so on.
- Review science safety rules.
- Review lab cleanup procedures.
- Have the needed materials available, organized, and set up for easy access.
- Monitor teams and provide productive feedback.
- Leave enough time at the end of class for cleanup and debriefing.
- Designate area for project storage.

Evaluation

Student Reflection: Students think about their team's choices for the design of the prototype. Students individually complete the "Reflection" handout.

Student Self-Evaluation: Students think about their behavior and performance as a team member. Students individually complete the "Self-Evaluation Rubric."

Lab Evaluation: The teacher completes the "Lab Challenge Rubric" for each team.

Conference: Teacher/student conferences are held to discuss the completed evaluations.

Rock and Mineral Identification Kit: Student Challenge

STEM Lab Challenge: Design a kit that can be used to perform a variety of physical property tests on rocks and minerals in the field or the classroom. The kit should include samples of common rocks and minerals and a detailed instruction manual.

You Should Know

Rock Cycle

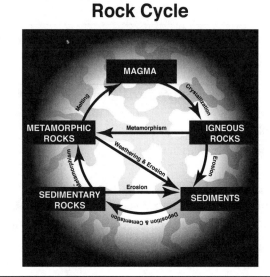

Vocabulary Review
- crystal
- rock
- mineral
- rock cycle

Materials You May Need
- streak plate
- copper penny
- glass plate
- nail
- magnet
- plastic bottle filled with vinegar
- hand lens
- guidebook for rocks and minerals
- other design materials: to be determined by student research

Challenge Requirements

1. <u>Research</u>: Write a one- to two-page paper summarizing your research on the rock cycle, rocks, minerals, and crystals. Cite your sources. Your paper may include two pictures.
2. <u>Model</u>: Label a drawing of kit contents. Explain the purpose of each item.
3. <u>Results</u>: Record, analyze, and interpret test results.
4. <u>Conclusion</u>: Summarize the lab and what actually happened. It should include the purpose, a brief description of the test procedure, and explanation of results.
5. <u>Reflection</u>: Think about your team's choices for the rock and mineral identification kit. Then complete the "Reflection" handout.
6. <u>Evaluation</u>: Think about your behavior and performance as a team member. Then complete the "Self-Evaluation Rubric."

Steps to Follow

Work with a team to complete the steps listed below. A team will have 3 or 4 members.

Step 1: Research the rock cycle, rocks, minerals, and crystals.

Step 2: Brainstorm ideas about how you might design a rock and mineral identification kit to meet the requirements of the lab. Think about the information that should be included in the instruction manual. Think about how users of the kit will record test results.

Step 3: Draw a diagram identifying the items in your kit and their purpose.

Step 4: Create the kit.

Step 5: Test the kit and record the results.

Step 6: Evaluate the performance of your rock and mineral identification kit.

Step 7: Identify how to improve your design.

Step 8: Make the needed changes.

Step 9: Retest and reevaluate your improved design.

Step 10: Share the results.

Soil Testing: Teacher Information

STEM Lab Overview
Students are challenged to design a system to collect and test pH levels of soil samples from various areas to determine the types of plants that would grow best in those locations.

Concepts
• Soil profile   • Types of soil   • Soil chemistry   • Nitrogen cycle

Standards for Grades 6–8			
NGSS	**NCTM**	**ITEA**	**CCSS**
-Earth's Systems	-Problem Solving -Communication -Connections -Representation	-Nature of Technology -Technology and Society -Technological World	-English Language Arts Standards: Science & Technical Subjects

Teaching Strategies
Step #1:   Engage—Review concepts. Introduce the STEM lab. Discuss the challenge presented in the lab, providing students with an opportunity to connect previous knowledge to the problem they are to solve. Step #2:   Investigate—Students conduct research to gain an understanding of the major science concepts related to the topic, review possible solutions to the lab challenge, and formulate new ideas for solving the problem. Step #3:   Explore—Students apply research to design and test a model, process, or system to solve the problem presented in the challenge. Step #4:   Communicate—Students share results. Step #5:   Evaluate—Students are given an opportunity to reflect on what they have learned.

Managing the Lab
• Set a deadline for project submission and presentations. • Group students into collaborative teams and assign roles. • Review prerequisite skills students need for doing the lab, such as measuring, weighing, constructing, recording data, graphing, and so on. • Review science safety rules. • Review lab cleanup procedures. • Have the needed materials available, organized, and set up for easy access. • Monitor teams and provide productive feedback. • Leave enough time at the end of class for cleanup and debriefing. • Designate area for project storage.

Evaluation
Student Reflection: Students think about their team's choices for the design of the prototype. Students individually complete the "Reflection" handout. Student Self-Evaluation: Students think about their behavior and performance as a team member. Students individually complete the "Self-Evaluation Rubric." Lab Evaluation: The teacher completes the "Lab Challenge Rubric" for each team. Conference: Teacher/student conferences are held to discuss the completed evaluations.

Geology

Soil Testing: Student Challenge

STEM Lab Challenge: Design a system to collect and test pH levels of soil samples from various areas to determine the types of plants that would grow best in those locations.

You Should Know

Soil is a valuable natural resource. All life on Earth depends on soil. Testing the soil using a pH-testing kit can determine its condition. The soil pH reflects whether a soil is acidic, neutral, or basic (alkaline). Changing the pH of a soil is frequently required to grow healthy plants.

Materials You May Need

- shovel
- supplies needed for a soil-test kit
- water
- plastic baggies
- other design materials: to be determined by student research

Vocabulary Review

- acidic
- alkaline
- basic
- horizons
- neutral
- nitrates
- phosphates
- potassium
- nitrogen cycle

Challenge Requirements

1. <u>Research</u>: Write a one- to two-page paper summarizing your research on pH levels and the best plants to grow in various soil types. Cite your sources. Your paper may include two pictures.
2. <u>Model</u>: Label a drawing of your soil-testing system and explain your strategy.
3. <u>Results</u>: Record, analyze, and interpret test results.
4. <u>Conclusion</u>: Summarize the lab and what actually happened. It should include the purpose, a brief description of the test procedure, and explanation of results.
5. <u>Reflection</u>: Think about your team's choices for the soil-testing system. Then complete the "Reflection" handout.
6. <u>Evaluation</u>: Think about your behavior and performance as a team member. Then complete the "Self-Evaluation Rubric."

Steps to Follow

Work with a team to complete the steps listed below. A team will have 3 or 4 members.

Step 1: Research pH levels and the best plants to grow in various soil types.

Step 2: Brainstorm ideas about how to design a process to meet the requirements of the lab. Think about how to map the locations of your soil samples. After testing soil samples, determine the types of plants that will grow best in each location.

Step 3: Draw a diagram of your system.

Step 4: Set up the system.

Step 5: Test the system and record the results.

Step 6: Evaluate the performance of your system.

Step 7: Identify how to improve your system.

Step 8: Make the needed changes.

Step 9: Retest and reevaluate your improved system.

Step 10: Share the results.

Cracks in the Earth: Teacher Information

STEM Lab Overview
Students are challenged to design three-dimensional models of the three primary types of faults (normal, reverse, strike-slip).

Concepts
• Interior structure of Earth   • Faults   • Plate tectonics

Standards for Grades 6–8

NGSS	NCTM	ITEA	CCSS
-Earth's Systems	-Problem Solving -Communication -Connections -Representation	-Nature of Technology -Technology and Society -Technological World	-English Language Arts Standards: Science & Technical Subjects

Teaching Strategies

Step #1:   Engage—Review concepts. Introduce the STEM lab. Discuss the challenge presented in the lab, providing students with an opportunity to connect previous knowledge to the problem they are to solve.

Step #2:   Investigate—Students conduct research to gain an understanding of the major science concepts related to the topic, review possible solutions to the lab challenge, and formulate new ideas for solving the problem.

Step #3:   Explore—Students apply research to design and test a model, process, or system to solve the problem presented in the challenge.

Step #4:   Communicate—Students share results.

Step #5:   Evaluate—Students are given an opportunity to reflect on what they have learned.

Managing the Lab

• Set a deadline for project submission and presentations.
• Group students into collaborative teams and assign roles.
• Review prerequisite skills students need for doing the lab, such as measuring, weighing, constructing, recording data, graphing, and so on.
• Review science safety rules.
• Review lab cleanup procedures.
• Have the needed materials available, organized, and set up for easy access.
• Monitor teams and provide productive feedback.
• Leave enough time at the end of class for cleanup and debriefing.
• Designate area for project storage.

Evaluation

Student Reflection: Students think about their team's choices for the design of the prototype. Students individually complete the "Reflection" handout.

Student Self-Evaluation: Students think about their behavior and performance as a team member. Students individually complete the "Self-Evaluation Rubric."

Lab Evaluation: The teacher completes the "Lab Challenge Rubric" for each team.

Conference: Teacher/student conferences are held to discuss the completed evaluations.

Geology

Cracks in the Earth: Student Challenge

STEM Lab Challenge: Design three-dimensional models of the three primary types of faults (normal, reverse, strike-slip).

You Should Know
You can think of Earth's surface as a giant puzzle with the tectonic plates as the pieces. The plates float like a raft on a lake on the layer of Earth called the mantle.

Vocabulary Review
- faults
- lithosphere
- mantle
- normal fault
- strike-slip fault
- tectonic plates
- thrust (reverse) fault

Fault Line

Materials You May Need
- design materials: to be determined by student research

Normal fault   Reverse fault   Strike-slip fault

Challenge Requirements
1. <u>Research</u>: Write a one- to two-page paper summarizing your research on plate tectonics and faults. Cite your sources. Your paper may include two pictures.
2. <u>Model</u>: Label a drawing of your three models. Explain your strategy.
3. <u>Results</u>: Record, analyze, and interpret test results.
4. <u>Conclusion</u>: Summarize the lab and what actually happened. It should include the purpose, a brief description of the test procedure, and explanation of results.
5. <u>Reflection</u>: Think about your team's choices for the models. Then complete the "Reflection" handout.
6. <u>Evaluation</u>: Think about your behavior and performance as a team member. Then complete the "Self-Evaluation Rubric."

Steps to Follow
Work with a team to complete the steps listed below. A team will have 3 or 4 members.

Step 1: Research plate tectonics and faults.
Step 2: Brainstorm ideas about how you might design the three models to meet the requirements of the lab.
Step 3: Draw a diagram of your designs.
Step 4: Construct the models.
Step 5: Test the accuracy of the designs by using your science book or other resources. Record the results of your comparisons.
Step 6: Evaluate how well the items chosen for your models actually meet the requirements of the lab.
Step 7: Identify how to improve your designs.
Step 8: Make the needed changes.
Step 9: Reevaluate your improved designs.
Step 10: Share the results.

Earthquake Simulator: Teacher Information

STEM Lab Overview

Students are challenged to design a wave simulator to demonstrate the damage caused during an earthquake.

Concepts

- Earthquake
- Seismic waves

Standards for Grades 6–8

NGSS	NCTM	ITEA	CCSS
-Earth's Systems	-Problem Solving -Communication -Connections -Representation	-Nature of Technology -Technology and Society -Technological World	-English Language Arts Standards: Science & Technical Subjects

Teaching Strategies

Step #1: Engage—Review concepts. Introduce the STEM lab. Discuss the challenge presented in the lab, providing students with an opportunity to connect previous knowledge to the problem they are to solve.

Step #2: Investigate—Students conduct research to gain an understanding of the major science concepts related to the topic, review possible solutions to the lab challenge, and formulate new ideas for solving the problem.

Step #3: Explore—Students apply research to design and test a model, process, or system to solve the problem presented in the challenge.

Step #4: Communicate—Students share results.

Step #5: Evaluate—Students are given an opportunity to reflect on what they have learned.

Managing the Lab

- Set a deadline for project submission and presentations.
- Group students into collaborative teams and assign roles.
- Review prerequisite skills students need for doing the lab, such as measuring, weighing, constructing, recording data, graphing, and so on.
- Review science safety rules.
- Review lab cleanup procedures.
- Have the needed materials available, organized, and set up for easy access.
- Monitor teams and provide productive feedback.
- Leave enough time at the end of class for cleanup and debriefing.
- Designate area for project storage.

Evaluation

Student Reflection: Students think about their team's choices for the design of the prototype. Students individually complete the "Reflection" handout.

Student Self-Evaluation: Students think about their behavior and performance as a team member. Students individually complete the "Self-Evaluation Rubric."

Lab Evaluation: The teacher completes the "Lab Challenge Rubric" for each team.

Conference: Teacher/student conferences are held to discuss the completed evaluations.

Earthquake Simulator: Student Challenge

STEM Lab Challenge: Design a wave simulator to demonstrate the damage caused during an earthquake.

You Should Know
Earthquakes produce two types of seismic waves—body waves and surface: P (primary) waves, S (secondary) waves.

Vocabulary Review
- earthquakes
- secondary waves
- surface waves
- primary waves
- seismic waves

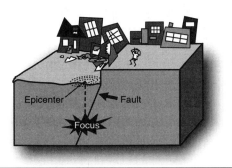

Epicenter   Fault

Focus

Materials You May Need
- materials to construct a primary shaker table
- small toy houses, people, cars, and animals
- other design materials: to be determined through student research

Challenge Requirements
1. <u>Research</u>: Write a one- to two-page paper summarizing your research on earthquakes and seismic waves. Cite your sources. Your paper may include two pictures.
2. <u>Model</u>: Label a drawing of your earthquake simulator. Explain your strategy.
3. <u>Results</u>: Record, analyze, and interpret test results.
4. <u>Conclusion</u>: Summarize the lab and what actually happened. It should include the purpose, a brief description of the test procedure, and explanation of results.
5. <u>Reflection</u>: Think about your team's choices for the earthquake simulator. Then complete the "Reflection" handout.
6. <u>Evaluation</u>: Think about your behavior and performance as a team member. Then complete the "Self-Evaluation Rubric."

Steps to Follow
Work with a team to complete the steps listed below. A team will have 3 or 4 members.

Step 1: Research earthquakes and seismic waves.
Step 2: Brainstorm ideas about how you might design a model of an earthquake simulator to meet the requirements of the lab.
Step 3: Draw a diagram of your simulator.
Step 4: Construct the model.
Step 5: Test the design and record the results.
Step 6: Evaluate the performance of your earthquake simulator.
Step 7: Identify how to improve your design.
Step 8: Make the needed changes.
Step 9: Retest and reevaluate your improved design.
Step 10: Share your results.

Stream Erosion and Deposition: Teacher Information

STEM Lab Overview

Students are challenged to design a working model of a stream system that demonstrates the process of sediment erosion, transportation, and deposition.

Concepts

- Erosion   • Deposition   • Sediment

Standards for Grades 6–8

NGSS	NCTM	ITEA	CCSS
-Earth's Systems	-Problem Solving -Communication -Connections -Representation	-Nature of Technology -Technology and Society -Technological World	-English Language Arts Standards: Science & Technical Subjects

Teaching Strategies

Step #1: Engage—Review concepts. Introduce the STEM lab. Discuss the challenge presented in the lab, providing students with an opportunity to connect previous knowledge to the problem they are to solve.

Step #2: Investigate—Students conduct research to gain an understanding of the major science concepts related to the topic, review possible solutions to the lab challenge, and formulate new ideas for solving the problem.

Step #3: Explore—Students apply research to design and test a model, process, or system to solve the problem presented in the challenge.

Step #4: Communicate—Students share results.

Step #5: Evaluate—Students are given an opportunity to reflect on what they have learned.

Managing the Lab

- Set a deadline for project submission and presentations.
- Group students into collaborative teams and assign roles.
- Review prerequisite skills students need for doing the lab, such as measuring, weighing, constructing, recording data, graphing, and so on.
- Review science safety rules.
- Review lab cleanup procedures.
- Have the needed materials available, organized, and set up for easy access.
- Monitor teams and provide productive feedback.
- Leave enough time at the end of class for cleanup and debriefing.
- Designate area for project storage.

Evaluation

<u>Student Reflection</u>: Students think about their team's choices for the design of the prototype. Students individually complete the "Reflection" handout.

<u>Student Self-Evaluation</u>: Students think about their behavior and performance as a team member. Students individually complete the "Self-Evaluation Rubric."

<u>Lab Evaluation</u>: The teacher completes the "Lab Challenge Rubric" for each team.

<u>Conference</u>: Teacher/student conferences are held to discuss the completed evaluations.

Geology

Stream Erosion and Deposition: Student Challenge

STEM Lab Challenge: Design a working model of a stream system that demonstrates the process of sediment erosion, transportation, and deposition.

You Should Know
Water moving through a stream system shapes the landscape. Water velocity is one of the main influences on a stream.

Vocabulary Review
- channel
- deposition
- erosion
- sediment
- streams
- velocity

Deposition
Erosion

Materials You May Need
- soil tray with holes
- large sink or container
- water faucet
- hose
- soil, clay, sand
- gravel
- other design materials: to be determined by student research

Challenge Requirements
1. Research: Write a one- to two-page paper summarizing your research on stream systems and the process of sediment erosion, transportation, and deposition. Cite your sources. Your paper may include two pictures.
2. Model: Label a drawing of your stream system model. Explain your strategy.
3. Results: Record, analyze, and interpret test results.
4. Conclusion: Summarize the lab and what actually happened. It should include the purpose, a brief description of the test procedure, and explanation of results.
5. Reflection: Think about your team's choices for the stream system model. Then complete the "Reflection" handout.
6. Evaluation: Think about your behavior and performance as a team member. Then complete the "Self-Evaluation Rubric."

Steps to Follow
Work with a team to complete the steps listed below. A team will have 3 or 4 members.

Step 1: Research stream systems and the process of sediment erosion, transportation, and deposition.
Step 2: Brainstorm ideas about how you might design your stream system model to meet the requirements of the lab. Think about how to position the tray to provide a constantly flowing stream and how to vary the velocity of the water flow.
Step 3: Draw a diagram of your system.
Step 4: Construct the model.
Step 5: Test the design and record the results.
Step 6: Evaluate the performance of your stream system.
Step 7: Identify how to improve your design.
Step 8: Make the needed changes.
Step 9: Retest and reevaluate your improved design.
Step 10: Share the results.

Cave Formation: Teacher Information

STEM Lab Overview
Students are challenged to design a working model of the cave formation process.

Concepts

• Groundwater	• Chemical weathering process

Standards for Grades 6–8

NGSS	NCTM	ITEA	CCSS
-Earth's Systems	-Problem Solving -Communication -Connections -Representation	-Nature of Technology -Technology and Society -Technological World	-English Language Arts Standards: Science & Technical Subjects

Teaching Strategies

Step #1: Engage—Review concepts. Introduce the STEM lab. Discuss the challenge presented in the lab, providing students with an opportunity to connect previous knowledge to the problem they are to solve.

Step #2: Investigate—Students conduct research to gain an understanding of the major science concepts related to the topic, review possible solutions to the lab challenge, and formulate new ideas for solving the problem.

Step #3: Explore—Students apply research to design and test a model, process, or system to solve the problem presented in the challenge.

Step #4: Communicate—Students share results.

Step #5: Evaluate—Students are given an opportunity to reflect on what they have learned.

Managing the Lab

• Set a deadline for project submission and presentations.
• Group students into collaborative teams and assign roles.
• Review prerequisite skills students need for doing the lab, such as measuring, weighing, constructing, recording data, graphing, and so on.
• Review science safety rules.
• Review lab cleanup procedures.
• Have the needed materials available, organized, and set up for easy access.
• Monitor teams and provide productive feedback.
• Leave enough time at the end of class for cleanup and debriefing.
• Designate area for project storage.

Evaluation

Student Reflection: Students think about their team's choices for the design of the prototype. Students individually complete the "Reflection" handout.

Student Self-Evaluation: Students think about their behavior and performance as a team member. Students individually complete the "Self-Evaluation Rubric."

Lab Evaluation: The teacher completes the "Lab Challenge Rubric" for each team.

Conference: Teacher/student conferences are held to discuss the completed evaluations.

Geology

Cave Formation: Student Challenge

STEM Lab Challenge: Design a working model of the cave formation process.

You Should Know

Caves form naturally by the process of chemical weathering. A cave begins to form when rainwater absorbs carbon dioxide in the ground and forms carbonic acid. The water seeps through cracks in limestone formations. This slowly dissolves the limestone. Over thousands of years, a large underground chamber is formed.

Vocabulary Review

- calcite
- carbonic acid
- erosion
- groundwater
- karst
- limestone
- sinkhole
- stalactite
- stalagmite
- weathering

Materials You May Need

- design materials: to be determined by student research

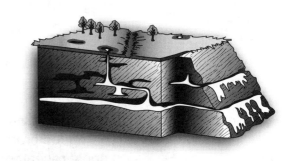

Challenge Requirements

1. <u>Research</u>: Write a one- to two-page paper summarizing your research on karst topography and cave formation. Cite your sources. Your paper may include two pictures.
2. <u>Model</u>: Label a drawing of your cave-formation model and explain your strategy.
3. <u>Results</u>: Record, analyze, and interpret test results.
4. <u>Conclusion</u>: Summarize the lab and what actually happened. It should include the purpose, a brief description of the test procedure, and explanation of results.
5. <u>Reflection</u>: Think about your team's choices for the cave-formation model. Then complete the "Reflection" handout.
6. <u>Evaluation</u>: Think about your behavior and performance as a team member. Then complete the "Self-Evaluation Rubric."

Steps to Follow

Work with a team to complete the steps listed below. A team will have 3 or 4 members.

Step 1: Research karst topography and cave formation.
Step 2: Brainstorm ideas about how to design a cave-formation model to meet the requirements of the lab.
Step 3: Draw a diagram of your cave-formation model.
Step 4: Construct the model.
Step 5: Test the design and record the results.
Step 6: Evaluate the performance of your cave-formation model.
Step 7: Identify how to improve your design.
Step 8: Make the needed changes.
Step 9: Retest and reevaluate your improved design.
Step 10: Share the results.

Well Water: Teacher Information

STEM Lab Overview

Students are challenged to design a model to demonstrate the relationship of groundwater to wells and show how pollutants can get into the groundwater.

Concepts

- Groundwater
- Water cycle
- Water table
- Wells

Standards for Grades 6–8

NGSS	NCTM	ITEA	CCSS
-Earth's Systems	-Problem Solving -Communication -Connections -Representation	-Nature of Technology -Technology and Society -Technological World	-English Language Arts Standards: Science & Technical Subjects

Teaching Strategies

Step #1: Engage—Review concepts. Introduce the STEM lab. Discuss the challenge presented in the lab, providing students with an opportunity to connect previous knowledge to the problem they are to solve.

Step #2: Investigate—Students conduct research to gain an understanding of the major science concepts related to the topic, review possible solutions to the lab challenge, and formulate new ideas for solving the problem.

Step #3: Explore—Students apply research to design and test a model, process, or system to solve the problem presented in the challenge.

Step #4: Communicate—Students share results.

Step #5: Evaluate—Students are given an opportunity to reflect on what they have learned.

Managing the Lab

- Set a deadline for project submission and presentations.
- Group students into collaborative teams and assign roles.
- Review prerequisite skills students need for doing the lab, such as measuring, weighing, constructing, recording data, graphing, and so on.
- Review science safety rules.
- Review lab cleanup procedures.
- Have the needed materials available, organized, and set up for easy access.
- Monitor teams and provide productive feedback.
- Leave enough time at the end of class for cleanup and debriefing.
- Designate area for project storage.

Evaluation

Student Reflection: Students think about their team's choices for the design of the prototype. Students individually complete the "Reflection" handout.

Student Self-Evaluation: Students think about their behavior and performance as a team member. Students individually complete the "Self-Evaluation Rubric."

Lab Evaluation: The teacher completes the "Lab Challenge Rubric" for each team.

Conference: Teacher/student conferences are held to discuss the completed evaluations.

Well Water: Student Challenge

STEM Lab Challenge: Design a model to demonstrate the relationship of groundwater to wells, and show how pollutants can get into the groundwater.

You Should Know

Groundwater comes from precipitation. As the water soaks into the soil, it moves downward to fill cracks and other openings in beds of rock and sand. Drilled wells tap into the groundwater and bring the water to the surface.

Vocabulary Review

- artesian well
- aquifer
- geyser
- groundwater
- impermeable
- permeable
- spring
- water table
- zone of saturation

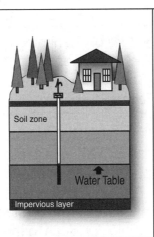

Soil zone

Water Table

Impervious layer

Materials You May Need

- design materials: to be determined by student research

Challenge Requirements

1. <u>Research</u>: Write a one- to two-page paper summarizing your research on groundwater, wells, and well pollutants. Cite your sources. Your paper may include two pictures.
2. <u>Model</u>: Label a drawing of your well model and explain your strategy.
3. <u>Results</u>: Record, analyze, and interpret test results.
4. <u>Conclusion</u>: Summarize the lab and what actually happened. It should include the purpose, a brief description of the test procedure, and explanation of results.
5. <u>Reflection</u>: Think about your team's choices for the well model. Then complete the "Reflection" handout.
6. <u>Evaluation</u>: Think about your behavior and performance as a team member. Then complete the "Self-Evaluation Rubric."

Steps to Follow

Work with a team to complete the steps listed below. A team will have 3 or 4 members.

Step 1: Research groundwater, wells, and well pollutants.
Step 2: Brainstorm ideas about how to design a well model to meet the requirements of the lab. Think about how to demonstrate what happens to the groundwater when you remove water from the well. Think about how to demonstrate what happens to your well as more water is added to the groundwater.
Step 3: Draw a diagram of your well model.
Step 4: Construct the model.
Step 5: Test the design and record the results.
Step 6: Evaluate the performance of your well model.
Step 7: Identify how to improve your design.
Step 8: Make the needed changes.
Step 9: Retest and reevaluate your design.
Step 10: Share the results.

Tide and Wave Erosion: Teacher Information

STEM Lab Overview

Students are challenged to design a tide and wave simulator to demonstrate the effects of erosion on an ocean shoreline.

Concepts

• Erosion   • Tides   • Waves

Standards for Grades 6–8

NGSS	NCTM	ITEA	CCSS
-Earth's Systems	-Problem Solving -Communication -Connections -Representation	-Nature of Technology -Technology and Society -Technological World	-English Language Arts Standards: Science & Technical Subjects

Teaching Strategies

Step #1:   Engage—Review concepts. Introduce the STEM lab. Discuss the challenge presented in the lab, providing students with an opportunity to connect previous knowledge to the problem they are to solve.

Step #2:   Investigate—Students conduct research to gain an understanding of the major science concepts related to the topic, review possible solutions to the lab challenge, and formulate new ideas for solving the problem.

Step #3:   Explore—Students apply research to design and test a model, process, or system to solve the problem presented in the challenge.

Step #4:   Communicate—Students share results.

Step #5:   Evaluate—Students are given an opportunity to reflect on what they have learned.

Managing the Lab

• Set a deadline for project submission and presentations.
• Group students into collaborative teams and assign roles.
• Review prerequisite skills students need for doing the lab, such as measuring, weighing, constructing, recording data, graphing, and so on.
• Review science safety rules.
• Review lab cleanup procedures.
• Have the needed materials available, organized, and set up for easy access.
• Monitor teams and provide productive feedback.
• Leave enough time at the end of class for cleanup and debriefing.
• Designate area for project storage.

Evaluation

Student Reflection: Students think about their team's choices for the design of the prototype. Students individually complete the "Reflection" handout.

Student Self-Evaluation: Students think about their behavior and performance as a team member. Students individually complete the "Self-Evaluation Rubric."

Lab Evaluation: The teacher completes the "Lab Challenge Rubric" for each team.

Conference: Teacher/student conferences are held to discuss the completed evaluations.

Tide and Wave Erosion: Student Challenge

STEM Lab Challenge: Design a tide and wave simulator to demonstrate the effects of erosion on an ocean shoreline.

You Should Know

People living at or near the ocean face the problem of coastal erosion. Entire coastlines are shaped by wave energy, especially sandy beaches, in a very short time period.

Vocabulary Review

- deposition
- erosion
- neap tide
- sea level
- sediment
- spring tide
- wave
- weathering

Materials You May Need

- large rectangular storage container
- sand
- water
- ruler
- other design materials: to be determined by student research

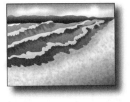

Challenge Requirements

1. <u>Research</u>: Write a one- to two-page paper summarizing your research on coastal erosion, waves, and tides. Cite your sources. Your paper may include two pictures.
2. <u>Model</u>: Label a drawing of your tide and wave simulator and explain your strategy.
3. <u>Results</u>: Record, analyze, and interpret test results.
4. <u>Conclusion</u>: Summarize the lab and what actually happened. It should include the purpose, a brief description of the test procedure, and explanation of results.
5. <u>Reflection</u>: Think about your team's choices for the tide and wave simulator. Then complete the "Reflection" handout.
6. <u>Evaluation</u>: Think about your behavior and performance as a team member. Then complete the "Self-Evaluation Rubric."

Steps to Follow

Work with a team to complete the steps listed below. A team will have 3 or 4 members.

Step 1: Research coastal erosion, waves, and tides.

Step 2: Brainstorm ideas about how to design a tide and wave simulator to meet the requirements of the lab.

Step 3: Draw a diagram of your simulator.

Step 4: Construct the model.

Step 5: Test the design and record the results.

Step 6: Evaluate the performance of your model.

Step 7: Identify how to improve your design.

Step 8: Make the needed changes.

Step 9: Retest and reevaluate your improved design.

Step 10: Share the results.

Seafloor Spreading and Subduction: Teacher Information

STEM Lab Overview

Students are challenged to design a model that illustrates the process of seafloor spreading and subduction.

Concepts to Review

- Continental drift   • Ocean   • Changes in the ocean floor

Standards for Grades 6–8

NGSS	NCTM	ITEA	CCSS
-Earth's Systems	-Problem Solving -Communication -Connections -Representation	-Nature of Technology -Technology and Society -Technological World	-English Language Arts Standards: Science & Technical Subjects

Teaching Strategies

Step #1: Engage—Review concepts. Introduce the STEM lab. Discuss the challenge presented in the lab, providing students with an opportunity to connect previous knowledge to the problem they are to solve.

Step #2: Investigate—Students conduct research to gain an understanding of the major science concepts related to the topic, review possible solutions to the lab challenge, and formulate new ideas for solving the problem.

Step #3: Explore—Students apply research to design and test a model, process, or system to solve the problem presented in the challenge.

Step #4: Communicate—Students share results.

Step #5: Evaluate—Students are given an opportunity to reflect on what they have learned.

Managing the Lab

- Set a deadline for project submission and presentations.
- Group students into collaborative teams and assign roles.
- Review prerequisite skills students need for doing the lab, such as measuring, weighing, constructing, recording data, graphing, and so on.
- Review science safety rules.
- Review lab cleanup procedures.
- Have the needed materials available, organized, and set up for easy access.
- Monitor teams and provide productive feedback.
- Leave enough time at the end of class for cleanup and debriefing.
- Designate area for project storage.

Evaluation

Student Reflection: Students think about their team's choices for the design of the prototype. Students individually complete the "Reflection" handout.

Student Self-Evaluation: Students think about their behavior and performance as a team member. Students individually complete the "Self-Evaluation Rubric."

Lab Evaluation: The teacher completes the "Lab Challenge Rubric" for each team.

Conference: Teacher/student conferences are held to discuss the completed evaluations.

Oceanography

Seafloor Spreading and Subduction: Student Challenge

STEM Lab Challenge: Design a model that illustrates the process of seafloor spreading and subduction.

You Should Know
Scientists believe that seafloor spreading explains the gradual movement of the continents across the earth's surface.

Materials You May Need
• design materials: to be determined by student research

Vocabulary Review
• continental crust
• continental drift
• deep-ocean floor
• deep-sea trench
• lithosphere
• mid-ocean ridge
• oceanic crust
• subduction

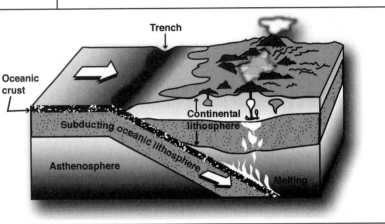

Challenge Requirements
1. <u>Research</u>: Write a one- to two-page paper summarizing your research on continental drift and seafloor spreading. Cite your sources. Your paper may include two pictures.
2. <u>Model</u>: Label a drawing of your model. Explain your strategy.
3. <u>Results</u>: Record, analyze, and interpret test results.
4. <u>Conclusion</u>: Summarize the lab and what actually happened. It should include the purpose, a brief description of the test procedure, and explanation of results.
5. <u>Reflection</u>: Think about your team's choices for the seafloor spreading model. Then complete the "Reflection" handout.
6. <u>Evaluation</u>: Think about your behavior and performance as a team member. Then complete the "Self-Evaluation Rubric."

Steps to Follow
Work with a team to complete the steps listed below. A team will have 3 or 4 members.

Step 1: Research continental drift and seafloor spreading.
Step 2: Brainstorm ideas about how you might design a model to Illustrate seafloor spreading and subduction to meet the requirements of the lab.
Step 3: Draw a diagram of your design.
Step 4: Construct the model.
Step 5: Test the accuracy of the design by using your science book or other resources. Record the results of your comparisons.
Step 6: Evaluate how well the items chosen for your model actually illustrate the process of seafloor spreading and subduction.
Step 7: Identify how to improve your design.
Step 8: Make the needed changes.
Step 9: Retest and reevaluate your improved design.
Step 10: Share the results.

Desalination System: Teacher Information

STEM Lab Overview
Students are challenged to design a desalination system to remove fresh water from salt water.

Concepts
• Water cycle   • Desalination

Standards for Grades 6–8			
NGSS	**NCTM**	**ITEA**	**CCSS**
-Earth's Systems	-Problem Solving -Communication -Connections -Representation	-Nature of Technology -Technology and Society -Technological World	-English Language Arts Standards: Science & Technical Subjects

Teaching Strategies

Step #1: Engage—Review concepts. Introduce the STEM lab. Discuss the challenge presented in the lab, providing students with an opportunity to connect previous knowledge to the problem they are to solve.

Step #2: Investigate—Students conduct research to gain an understanding of the major science concepts related to the topic, review possible solutions to the lab challenge, and formulate new ideas for solving the problem.

Step #3: Explore—Students apply research to design and test a model, process, or system to solve the problem presented in the challenge.

Step #4: Communicate—Students share results.

Step #5: Evaluate—Students are given an opportunity to reflect on what they have learned.

Managing the Lab

• Set a deadline for project submission and presentations.
• Group students into collaborative teams and assign roles.
• Review prerequisite skills students need for doing the lab, such as measuring, weighing, constructing, recording data, graphing, and so on.
• Review science safety rules.
• Review lab cleanup procedures.
• Have the needed materials available, organized, and set up for easy access.
• Monitor teams and provide productive feedback.
• Leave enough time at the end of class for cleanup and debriefing.
• Designate area for project storage.

Evaluation

Student Reflection: Students think about their team's choices for the design of the prototype. Students individually complete the "Reflection" handout.

Student Self-Evaluation: Students think about their behavior and performance as a team member. Students individually complete the "Self-Evaluation Rubric."

Lab Evaluation: The teacher completes the "Lab Challenge Rubric" for each team.

Conference: Teacher/student conferences are held to discuss the completed evaluations.

Oceanography

Desalination System: Student Challenge

STEM Lab Challenge: Design a desalination system to remove fresh water from salt water.

You Should Know
The total amount of safe drinking water available on our planet is less than one percent of all water.

Vocabulary Review
- condensation
- conductivity tester
- density
- electrodes
- evaporation
- ions
- molecules
- salinity
- desalination
- water cycle
- water vapor

Materials You May Need
- pan balance
- conductivity tester
- table salt
- water
- ice
- beakers and flasks
- shallow pan
- hot plate
- rubber tubing
- thermal mitts and safety goggles
- other design materials: to be determined by student research

Challenge Requirements
1. <u>Research</u>: Write a one- to two-page paper summarizing your research on ocean water desalination. Cite your sources. Your paper may include two pictures.
2. <u>Model</u>: Label a drawing of your desalination system and explain your strategy.
3. <u>Results</u>: Record, analyze, and interpret test results.
4. <u>Conclusion</u>: Summarize the lab and what actually happened. It should include the purpose, a brief description of the test procedure, and explanation of results.
5. <u>Reflection</u>: Think about your team's choices for the desalination system. Then complete the "Reflection" handout.
6. <u>Evaluation</u>: Think about your behavior and performance as a team member. Then complete the "Self-Evaluation Rubric."

Steps to Follow
Work with a team to complete the steps listed below. A team will have 3 or 4 members.

Step 1: Research ocean water desalination.
Step 2: Brainstorm ideas about how to design a desalination system to meet the requirements of the lab.
Step 3: Draw a diagram of your system.
Step 4: Set up the system.
Step 5: Test the system and record the results.
Step 6: Evaluate the performance of your system.
Step 7: Identify how to improve the design of your system.
Step 8: Make the needed changes.
Step 9: Retest and reevaluate your improved system.
Step 10: Share the results.

Oceanography

Tsunamis and Coastal Homes: Teacher Information

STEM Lab Overview
Students are challenged to design a tsunami generator to demonstrate the effects of tsunamis on coastal homes.

Concepts
• Plate tectonics   • Earthquakes   • Volcanoes   • Waves

Standards for Grades 6–8

NGSS	NCTM	ITEA	CCSS
-Earth's Systems	-Problem Solving -Communication -Connections -Representation	-Nature of Technology -Technology and Society -Technological World	-English Language Arts Standards: Science & Technical Subjects

Teaching Strategies

Step #1:   Engage—Review concepts. Introduce the STEM lab. Discuss the challenge presented in the lab, providing students with an opportunity to connect previous knowledge to the problem they are to solve.

Step #2:   Investigate—Students conduct research to gain an understanding of the major science concepts related to the topic, review possible solutions to the lab challenge, and formulate new ideas for solving the problem.

Step #3:   Explore—Students apply research to design and test a model, process, or system to solve the problem presented in the challenge.

Step #4:   Communicate—Students share results.

Step #5:   Evaluate—Students are given an opportunity to reflect on what they have learned.

Managing the Lab

- Set a deadline for project submission and presentations.
- Group students into collaborative teams and assign roles.
- Review prerequisite skills students need for doing the lab, such as measuring, weighing, constructing, recording data, graphing, and so on.
- Review science safety rules.
- Review lab cleanup procedures.
- Have the needed materials available, organized, and set up for easy access.
- Monitor teams and provide productive feedback.
- Leave enough time at the end of class for cleanup and debriefing.
- Designate area for project storage.

Evaluation

Student Reflection: Students think about their team's choices for the design of the prototype. Students individually complete the "Reflection" handout.

Student Self-Evaluation: Students think about their behavior and performance as a team member. Students individually complete the "Self-Evaluation Rubric."

Lab Evaluation: The teacher completes the "Lab Challenge Rubric" for each team.

Conference: Teacher/student conferences are held to discuss the completed evaluations.

Tsunamis and Coastal Homes: Student Challenge

STEM Lab Challenge: Design a tsunami generator to demonstrate the effects of tsunamis on coastal homes.

You Should Know

A tsunami is a series of gigantic waves caused by earthquakes beneath the ocean floor or by underwater landslides or volcanic eruptions and other underwater explosions. The powerful waves of a tsunami can move as quickly as a jet plane and destroy everything along the coastline.

Vocabulary Review

- amplitude
- crest
- seismograph
- trough
- waves
- continental shelf
- earthquake focus
- surge
- tsunami

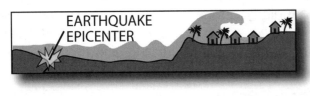

Materials You May Need

- long plastic storage container
- sand
- water
- cardboard
- scissors
- other design materials: to be determined by student research

Challenge Requirements

1. <u>Research</u>: Write a one- to two-page paper summarizing your research on tsunamis and coastal housing. Cite your sources. Your paper may include two pictures.
2. <u>Model</u>: Label a drawing of your tsunami generator model and explain your strategy.
3. <u>Results</u>: Record, analyze, and interpret test results.
4. <u>Conclusion</u>: Summarize the lab and what actually happened. It should include the purpose, a brief description of the test procedure, and explanation of results.
5. <u>Reflection</u>: Think about your team's choices for the tsunami generator model. Then complete the "Reflection" handout.
6. <u>Evaluation</u>: Think about your behavior and performance as a team member. Then complete the "Self-Evaluation Rubric."

Steps to Follow

Work with a team to complete the steps listed below. A team will have 3 or 4 members.

Step 1: Research tsunamis and coastal housing.

Step 2: Brainstorm ideas about how to design a model to meet the requirements of the lab. Think about the materials you will use to construct the houses.

Step 3: Draw a diagram of your design.

Step 4: Construct the tsunami generator.

Step 5: Test the design and record the results.

Step 6: Evaluate the performance of your tsunami generator.

Step 7: Identify how to improve your design.

Step 8: Make the needed changes.

Step 9: Retest and reevaluate your improved design.

Step 10: Share the results.

Weather Station: Teacher Information

STEM Lab Overview
Students are challenged to design a weather station with homemade weather instruments to measure air pressure, wind speed and direction, temperature, precipitation, and relative humidity to predict future weather conditions.

Concepts
• Weather   • Weather instruments

Standards for Grades 6–8

NGSS	NCTM	ITEA	CCSS
-Weather and Climate	-Problem Solving -Communication -Connections -Representation	-Nature of Technology -Technology and Society -Technological World	-English Language Arts Standards: Science & Technical Subjects

Teaching Strategies

Step #1: Engage—Review concepts. Introduce the STEM lab. Discuss the challenge presented in the lab, providing students with an opportunity to connect previous knowledge to the problem they are to solve.

Step #2: Investigate—Students conduct research to gain an understanding of the major science concepts related to the topic, review possible solutions to the lab challenge, and formulate new ideas for solving the problem.

Step #3: Explore—Students apply research to design and test a model, process, or system to solve the problem presented in the challenge.

Step #4: Communicate—Students share results.

Step #5: Evaluate—Students are given an opportunity to reflect on what they have learned.

Managing the Lab

• Set a deadline for project submission and presentations.
• Group students into collaborative teams and assign roles.
• Review prerequisite skills students need for doing the lab, such as measuring, weighing, constructing, recording data, graphing, and so on.
• Review science safety rules.
• Review lab cleanup procedures.
• Have the needed materials available, organized, and set up for easy access.
• Monitor teams and provide productive feedback.
• Leave enough time at the end of class for cleanup and debriefing.
• Designate area for project storage.

Evaluation

Student Reflection: Students think about their team's choices for the design of the prototype. Students individually complete the "Reflection" handout.
Student Self-Evaluation: Students think about their behavior and performance as a team member. Students individually complete the "Self-Evaluation Rubric."
Lab Evaluation: The teacher completes the "Lab Challenge Rubric" for each team.
Conference: Teacher/student conferences are held to discuss the completed evaluations.

Weather Station: Student Challenge

STEM Lab Challenge: Design a weather station with homemade weather instruments to measure air pressure, wind speed and direction, temperature, precipitation, and relative humidity to predict future weather conditions.

You Should Know
A weather station is a place where scientists observe, measure, and record weather conditions.

Vocabulary Review
- anemometer
- barometer
- hygrometer
- rain gauge
- thermometer
- weather
- wind vane

Materials You May Need
- design materials: to be determined by student research

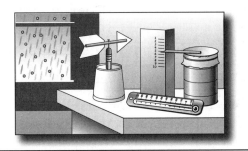

Challenge Requirements
1. <u>Research</u>: Write a one- to two-page paper summarizing your research on weather and homemade weather instruments. Cite your sources. Your paper may include two pictures.
2. <u>Model</u>: Label a drawing of your weather station and explain your strategy.
3. <u>Results</u>: Record, analyze, and interpret test results.
4. <u>Conclusion</u>: Summarize the lab and what actually happened. It should include the purpose, a brief description of the test procedure, and explanation of results.
5. <u>Reflection</u>: Think about your team's choices for the weather station. Then complete the "Reflection" handout.
6. <u>Evaluation</u>: Think about your behavior and performance as a team member. Then complete the "Self-Evaluation Rubric."

Steps to Follow
Work with a team to complete the steps listed below. A team will have 3 or 4 members.

Step 1: Research weather and homemade weather instruments.

Step 2: Brainstorm ideas about how to design a weather station to meet the requirements of the lab. Think about the materials you will use to make your weather instruments.

Step 3: Draw a diagram of your weather station and instruments.

Step 4: Construct the instruments for the weather station.

Step 5: Test the weather instruments and record the results.

Step 6: Evaluate the performance of your weather station.

Step 7: Identify how to improve the design of your weather instruments.

Step 8: Make the needed changes.

Step 9: Retest and reevaluate your improved weather station design.

Step 10: Share the results.

Fog to Water: Teacher Information

STEM Lab Overview

Students are challenged to design a system to collect fresh water from fog without using electricity.

Concepts

- Water cycle   • Clouds   • Weather

Standards for Grades 6–8			
NGSS	**NCTM**	**ITEA**	**CCSS**
-Weather and Climate	-Problem Solving -Communication -Connections -Representation	-Nature of Technology -Technology and Society -Technological World	-English Language Arts Standards: Science & Technical Subjects

Teaching Strategies

Step #1:   Engage—Review concepts. Introduce the STEM lab. Discuss the challenge presented in the lab, providing students with an opportunity to connect previous knowledge to the problem they are to solve.

Step #2:   Investigate—Students conduct research to gain an understanding of the major science concepts related to the topic, review possible solutions to the lab challenge, and formulate new ideas for solving the problem.

Step #3:   Explore—Students apply research to design and test a model, process, or system to solve the problem presented in the challenge.

Step #4:   Communicate—Students share results.

Step #5:   Evaluate—Students are given an opportunity to reflect on what they have learned.

Managing the Lab

- Set a deadline for project submission and presentations.
- Group students into collaborative teams and assign roles.
- Review prerequisite skills students need for doing the lab, such as measuring, weighing, constructing, recording data, graphing, and so on.
- Review science safety rules.
- Review lab cleanup procedures.
- Have the needed materials available, organized, and set up for easy access.
- Monitor teams and provide productive feedback.
- Leave enough time at the end of class for cleanup and debriefing.
- Designate area for project storage.

Evaluation

Student Reflection: Students think about their team's choices for the design of the prototype. Students individually complete the "Reflection" handout.

Student Self-Evaluation: Students think about their behavior and performance as a team member. Students individually complete the "Self-Evaluation Rubric."

Lab Evaluation: The teacher completes the "Lab Challenge Rubric" for each team.

Conference: Teacher/student conferences are held to discuss the completed evaluations.

Meteorology

Fog to Water: Student Challenge

STEM Lab Challenge: Design a system to collect fresh water from fog without using electricity.

You Should Know

Fog collectors are being used in areas where water is scarce. Fog condenses on a special plastic mesh and forms water droplets. The water then flows down toward a trough and into a reservoir.

Vocabulary Review

- atmospheric water vapor
- clouds
- condensation
- dew
- dew point
- evaporation
- fog
- humidity
- precipitation
- prevailing winds

Materials You May Need

- design materials: to be determined by student research

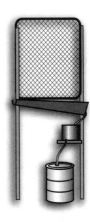

Challenge Requirements

1. <u>Research</u>: Write a one- to two-page paper summarizing your research on fog water collectors. Cite your sources. Your paper may include two pictures.
2. <u>Model</u>: Label a drawing of your fog-collector system and explain your strategy.
3. <u>Results</u>: Record, analyze, and interpret test results.
4. <u>Conclusion</u>: Summarize the lab and what actually happened. It should include the purpose, a brief description of the test procedure, and explanation of results.
5. <u>Reflection</u>: Think about your team's choices for the fog-collector system. Then complete the "Reflection" handout.
6. <u>Evaluation</u>: Think about your behavior and performance as a team member. Then complete the "Self-Evaluation Rubric."

Steps to Follow

Work with a team to complete the steps listed below. A team will have 3 or 4 members.

Step 1: Research fog water collectors.
Step 2: Brainstorm ideas about how to design a fog-collector system to meet the requirements of the lab. Think about the kind of material you will use to capture the fog.
Step 3: Draw a diagram of your fog-collector system.
Step 4: Construct the fog-collector system.
Step 5: Test the system and record the results.
Step 6: Evaluate the performance of your fog-collector system.
Step 7: Identify how to improve your design.
Step 8: Make the needed changes.
Step 9: Retest and reevaluate your improved system.
Step 10: Share the results.

Dew and Frost Maker: Teacher Information

STEM Lab Overview
Students are challenged to design a device to demonstrate how dew and frost are formed.

Concepts
• Dew   • Frost

Standards for Grades 6–8

NGSS	NCTM	ITEA	CCSS
-Weather and Climate	-Problem Solving -Communication -Connections -Representation	-Nature of Technology -Technology and Society -Technological World	-English Language Arts Standards: Science & Technical Subjects

Teaching Strategies

Step #1: Engage—Review concepts. Introduce the STEM lab. Discuss the challenge presented in the lab, providing students with an opportunity to connect previous knowledge to the problem they are to solve.

Step #2: Investigate—Students conduct research to gain an understanding of the major science concepts related to the topic, review possible solutions to the lab challenge, and formulate new ideas for solving the problem.

Step #3: Explore—Students apply research to design and test a model, process, or system to solve the problem presented in the challenge.

Step #4: Communicate—Students share results.

Step #5: Evaluate—Students are given an opportunity to reflect on what they have learned.

Managing the Lab

- Set a deadline for project submission and presentations.
- Group students into collaborative teams and assign roles.
- Review prerequisite skills students need for doing the lab, such as measuring, weighing, constructing, recording data, graphing, and so on.
- Review science safety rules.
- Review lab cleanup procedures.
- Have the needed materials available, organized, and set up for easy access.
- Monitor teams and provide productive feedback.
- Leave enough time at the end of class for cleanup and debriefing.
- Designate area for project storage.

Evaluation

Student Reflection: Students think about their team's choices for the design of the prototype. Students individually complete the "Reflection" handout.

Student Self-Evaluation: Students think about their behavior and performance as a team member. Students individually complete the "Self-Evaluation Rubric."

Lab Evaluation: The teacher completes the "Lab Challenge Rubric" for each team.

Conference: Teacher/student conferences are held to discuss the completed evaluations.

Dew and Frost Maker: Student Challenge

STEM Lab Challenge: Design a device to demonstrate how dew and frost are formed.

You Should Know
Air contains water vapor; when it condenses on windows, cars, and grass, it is called dew. If the surface is below the freezing point of water, the condensed water vapor freezes, and frost is formed.

Vocabulary Review
- air temperature
- condensation
- dew
- dew point
- evaporation
- frost
- humidity
- psychrometer
- relative humidity
- saturation
- water vapor

Materials You May Need
- two soup cans with labels removed
- crushed ice
- salt
- water
- thermometer
- other design materials: to be determined by student research

Challenge Requirements
1. <u>Research</u>: Write a one- to two-page paper summarizing your research on dew and frost. Cite your sources. Your paper may include two pictures.
2. <u>Model</u>: Label a drawing of your dew and frost maker and explain your strategy.
3. <u>Results</u>: Record, analyze, and interpret test results.
4. <u>Conclusion</u>: Summarize the lab and what actually happened. It should include the purpose, a brief description of the test procedure, and explanation of results.
5. <u>Reflection</u>: Think about your team's choices for the dew and frost maker. Then complete the "Reflection" handout.
6. <u>Evaluation</u>: Think about your behavior and performance as a team member. Then complete the "Self-Evaluation Rubric."

Steps to Follow
Work with a team to complete the steps listed below. A team will have 3 or 4 members.

Step 1: Research dew and frost.
Step 2: Brainstorm ideas about how to design a model to meet the requirements of the lab.
Step 3: Draw a diagram of your design.
Step 4: Construct the dew and frost maker.
Step 5: Test the design and record the results.
Step 6: Evaluate the performance of your dew and frost maker.
Step 7: Identify how to improve your design.
Step 8: Make the needed changes.
Step 9: Retest and reevaluate your improved design.
Step 10: Share the results.

Mini Water Cycle: Teacher Information

STEM Lab Overview

Students are challenged to design a model that demonstrates the water cycle process.

Concepts

- Water cycle
- Weather

Standards for Grades 6–8

NGSS	NCTM	ITEA	CCSS
-Weather and Climate	-Problem Solving -Communication -Connections -Representation	-Nature of Technology -Technology and Society -Technological World	-English Language Arts Standards: Science & Technical Subjects

Teaching Strategies

Step #1: Engage—Review concepts. Introduce the STEM lab. Discuss the challenge presented in the lab, providing students with an opportunity to connect previous knowledge to the problem they are to solve.

Step #2: Investigate—Students conduct research to gain an understanding of the major science concepts related to the topic, review possible solutions to the lab challenge, and formulate new ideas for solving the problem.

Step #3: Explore—Students apply research to design and test a model, process, or system to solve the problem presented in the challenge.

Step #4: Communicate—Students share results.

Step #5: Evaluate—Students are given an opportunity to reflect on what they have learned.

Managing the Lab

- Set a deadline for project submission and presentations.
- Group students into collaborative teams and assign roles.
- Review prerequisite skills students need for doing the lab, such as measuring, weighing, constructing, recording data, graphing, and so on.
- Review science safety rules.
- Review lab cleanup procedures.
- Have the needed materials available, organized, and set up for easy access.
- Monitor teams and provide productive feedback.
- Leave enough time at the end of class for cleanup and debriefing.
- Designate area for project storage.

Evaluation

Student Reflection: Students think about their team's choices for the design of the prototype. Students individually complete the "Reflection" handout.

Student Self-Evaluation: Students think about their behavior and performance as a team member. Students individually complete the "Self-Evaluation Rubric."

Lab Evaluation: The teacher completes the "Lab Challenge Rubric" for each team.

Conference: Teacher/student conferences are held to discuss the completed evaluations.

Meteorology

Mini Water Cycle: Student Challenge

STEM Lab Challenge: Design a model that demonstrates the water cycle process.

You Should Know

The sun heats the earth, causing water to evaporate and rise into the sky. The water vapor collects, forming clouds. Water falls back to the earth in the form of rain, freezing rain, sleet, snow, or hail.

Materials You May Need

- dry ceramic coffee mug
- large metal bowl
- large rubber band
- sheet of clear plastic wrap
- water
- other design materials: to be determined by student research

Vocabulary Review

- clouds
- evaporation
- water cycle
- condensation
- precipitation
- weather

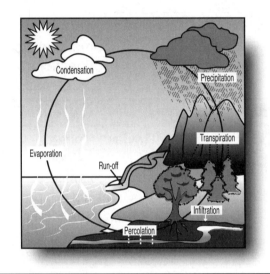

Challenge Requirements

1. <u>Research</u>: Write a one- to two-page paper summarizing your research on weather and the water cycle. Cite your sources. Your paper may include two pictures.
2. <u>Model</u>: Label a drawing of your water cycle model. Explain your strategy.
3. <u>Results</u>: Record, analyze, and interpret test results.
4. <u>Conclusion</u>: Summarize the lab and what actually happened. It should include the purpose, a brief description of the test procedure, and explanation of results.
5. <u>Reflection</u>: Think about your team's choices for the water cycle model. Then complete the "Reflection" handout.
6. <u>Evaluation</u>: Think about your behavior and performance as a team member. Then complete the "Self-Evaluation Rubric."

Steps to Follow

Work with a team to complete the steps listed below. A team will have 3 or 4 members.

Step 1: Research weather and the water cycle.

Step 2: Brainstorm ideas about how you might design a model of the water cycle to meet the requirements of the lab.

Step 3: Draw a diagram of your water cycle design.

Step 4: Construct the model.

Step 5: Test the design and record the results.

Step 6: Evaluate the performance of your water cycle model.

Step 7: Identify how to improve your design.

Step 8: Make the needed changes.

Step 9: Retest and reevaluate your improved design.

Step 10: Share the results.

Family Flood Preparedness: Teacher Information

STEM Lab Overview
Students are challenged to design a flood disaster plan and supply kit for their family.

Concepts

• Rainfall	• Floods	• Floodplain	• Water cycle

Standards for Grades 6–8

NGSS	NCTM	ITEA	CCSS
-Weather and Climate	-Problem Solving -Communication -Connections -Representation	-Nature of Technology -Technology and Society -Technological World	-English Language Arts Standards: Science & Technical Subjects

Teaching Strategies

Step #1: Engage—Review concepts. Introduce the STEM lab. Discuss the challenge presented in the lab, providing students with an opportunity to connect previous knowledge to the problem they are to solve.

Step #2: Investigate—Students conduct research to gain an understanding of the major science concepts related to the topic, review possible solutions to the lab challenge, and formulate new ideas for solving the problem.

Step #3: Explore—Students apply research to design and test a model, process, or system to solve the problem presented in the challenge.

Step #4: Communicate—Students share results.

Step #5: Evaluate—Students are given an opportunity to reflect on what they have learned.

Managing the Lab

• Set a deadline for project submission and presentations.
• Group students into collaborative teams and assign roles.
• Review prerequisite skills students need for doing the lab, such as measuring, weighing, constructing, recording data, graphing, and so on.
• Review science safety rules.
• Review lab cleanup procedures.
• Have the needed materials available, organized, and set up for easy access.
• Monitor teams and provide productive feedback.
• Leave enough time at the end of class for cleanup and debriefing.
• Designate area for project storage.

Evaluation

Student Reflection: Students think about their team's choices for the design of the prototype. Students individually complete the "Reflection" handout.

Student Self-Evaluation: Students think about their behavior and performance as a team member. Students individually complete the "Self-Evaluation Rubric."

Lab Evaluation: The teacher completes the "Lab Challenge Rubric" for each team.

Conference: Teacher/student conferences are held to discuss the completed evaluations.

Family Flood Preparedness: Student Challenge

STEM Lab Challenge: Design a flood disaster plan and supply kit for your family.

You Should Know

Flooding is the most common natural weather event. Floods can happen in every U.S. state. They occur during heavy rains, when rivers or lakes overflow, when snow melts too fast, when ocean waves come ashore, or when levees or dams break. Creating a family disaster plan and disaster supply kit will help you prepare for a flooding emergency.

Vocabulary Review

- dam
- flash flood
- floodplain
- flood warning
- flood watch
- levee
- rainfall
- water cycle

Materials You May Need

- design materials: to be determined by student research and geographical location

Steps to Follow

Work with a team to complete the steps listed below. A team will have 3 or 4 members.

Step 1: Research flooding and flood disaster kits.

Step 2: Brainstorm ideas about how to design a family disaster flood plan and supply kit to meet the requirements of the lab. Think about a place to meet outside your neighborhood in case you cannot return to your home, the address and phone numbers everyone will need, and how to care for your pets.

Step 3: Write your plan and make a list of supplies needed for your kit.

Step 4: Go online to the American Red Cross web site. Click on "Types of Disasters" and scroll down and click on "Floods." Use the information found there to improve your plan and kit.

Step 5: Make the needed changes.

Step 6: Reevaluate your improved plan and supply kit.

Step 7: Share the results.

Challenge Requirements

1. <u>Research</u>: Write a one- to two-page paper summarizing your research on flooding and flood disaster kits. Cite your sources. Your paper may include two pictures.
2. <u>Model</u>: Label a drawing of your supply kit and explain your flood plan strategy.
3. <u>Results</u>: Record, analyze, and interpret test results.
4. <u>Conclusion</u>: Summarize the lab and what actually happened. It should include the purpose, a brief description of the test procedure, and explanation of results.
5. <u>Reflection</u>: Think about your team's choices for the flood plan and supply kit. Then complete the "Reflection" handout.
6. <u>Evaluation</u>: Think about your behavior and performance as a team member. Then complete the "Self-Evaluation Rubric."

Distances in Our Solar System: Teacher Information

STEM Lab Overview
Students are challenged to design a scale model of our solar system.

Concepts
• Astronomical units (AU)   • Our solar system

Standards for Grades 6–8			
NGSS	**NCTM**	**ITEA**	**CCSS**
-Space Systems	-Problem Solving -Communication -Connections -Representation	-Nature of Technology -Technology and Society -Technological World	-English Language Arts Standards: Science & Technical Subjects

Teaching Strategies
Step #1: Engage—Review concepts. Introduce the STEM lab. Discuss the challenge presented in the lab, providing students with an opportunity to connect previous knowledge to the problem they are to solve. Step #2: Investigate—Students conduct research to gain an understanding of the major science concepts related to the topic, review possible solutions to the lab challenge, and formulate new ideas for solving the problem. Step #3: Explore—Students apply research to design and test a model, process, or system to solve the problem presented in the challenge. Step #4: Communicate—Students share results. Step #5: Evaluate—Students are given an opportunity to reflect on what they have learned.

Managing the Lab
• Set a deadline for project submission and presentations. • Group students into collaborative teams and assign roles. • Review prerequisite skills students need for doing the lab, such as measuring, weighing, constructing, recording data, graphing, and so on. • Review science safety rules. • Review lab cleanup procedures. • Have the needed materials available, organized, and set up for easy access. • Monitor teams and provide productive feedback. • Leave enough time at the end of class for cleanup and debriefing. • Designate area for project storage.

Evaluation
<u>Student Reflection</u>: Students think about their team's choices for the design of the prototype. Students individually complete the "Reflection" handout. <u>Student Self-Evaluation</u>: Students think about their behavior and performance as a team member. Students individually complete the "Self-Evaluation Rubric." <u>Lab Evaluation</u>: The teacher completes the "Lab Challenge Rubric" for each team. <u>Conference</u>: Teacher/student conferences are held to discuss the completed evaluations.

Astronomy

Distances in Our Solar System: Student Challenge

STEM Lab Challenge: Design a scale model of our solar system.

You Should Know
The sizes of the planets vary greatly as do the distances between planets and their distance from the sun. Scientists use astronomical units (AU) when measuring distances in the solar system.

Vocabulary Review
- astronomical units (AU)
- planets
- solar system
- sun

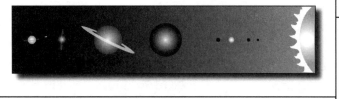

Materials You May Need
- adding-machine tape
- colored construction paper
- colored markers
- meter stick
- scissors
- string
- other design materials: to be determined by student research

Steps to Follow
Work with a team to complete the steps listed below. A team will have 3 or 4 members.

Step 1: Research astronomical units and our solar system.

Step 2: Brainstorm ideas about how you might design a scale model of our solar system. Think about how you can use astronomical units to make the model.

Step 3: Draw a diagram of your design.

Step 4: Construct the model.

Step 5: Test the accuracy of the design by using your science book or other resources. Check your calculations of the distances between the sun and the planets of our solar system. Record the results.

Step 6: Evaluate how well your scale model represents the solar system.

Step 7: Identify how to improve your design.

Step 8: Make the needed changes.

Step 9: Retest and reevaluate your improved design.

Step 10: Share the results.

Challenge Requirements
1. <u>Research</u>: Write a one- to two-page paper summarizing your research on astronomical units and our solar system. Cite your sources. Your paper may include two pictures.
2. <u>Model</u>: Label a drawing of your model and explain your strategy.
3. <u>Results</u>: Record, analyze, and interpret test results.
4. <u>Conclusion</u>: Summarize the lab and what actually happened. It should include the purpose, a brief description of the test procedure, and explanation of results.
5. <u>Reflection</u>: Think about your team's choices for the solar system model. Then complete the "Reflection" handout.
6. <u>Evaluation</u>: Think about your behavior and performance as a team member. Then complete the "Self-Evaluation Rubric."

The Earth-Sun System: Teacher Information

STEM Lab Overview

Students are challenged to design a 3-dimensional model of the Earth-sun system. The model should demonstrate the effect of rotation on sunrise, noon, sunset, and midnight.

Concepts

- Earth-sun system   • Day   • Night

Standards for Grades 6–8

NGSS	NCTM	ITEA	CCSS
-Space Systems	-Problem Solving -Communication -Connections -Representation	-Nature of Technology -Technology and Society -Technological World	-English Language Arts Standards: Science & Technical Subjects

Teaching Strategies

Step #1: Engage—Review concepts. Introduce the STEM lab. Discuss the challenge presented in the lab, providing students with an opportunity to connect previous knowledge to the problem they are to solve.

Step #2: Investigate—Students conduct research to gain an understanding of the major science concepts related to the topic, review possible solutions to the lab challenge, and formulate new ideas for solving the problem.

Step #3: Explore—Students apply research to design and test a model, process, or system to solve the problem presented in the challenge.

Step #4: Communicate—Students share results.

Step #5: Evaluate—Students are given an opportunity to reflect on what they have learned.

Managing the Lab

- Set a deadline for project submission and presentations.
- Group students into collaborative teams and assign roles.
- Review prerequisite skills students need for doing the lab, such as measuring, weighing, constructing, recording data, graphing, and so on.
- Review science safety rules.
- Review lab cleanup procedures.
- Have the needed materials available, organized, and set up for easy access.
- Monitor teams and provide productive feedback.
- Leave enough time at the end of class for cleanup and debriefing.
- Designate area for project storage.

Evaluation

<u>Student Reflection</u>: Students think about their team's choices for the design of the prototype. Students individually complete the "Reflection" handout.

<u>Student Self-Evaluation</u>: Students think about their behavior and performance as a team member. Students individually complete the "Self-Evaluation Rubric."

<u>Lab Evaluation</u>: The teacher completes the "Lab Challenge Rubric" for each team.

<u>Conference</u>: Teacher/student conferences are held to discuss the completed evaluations.

The Earth-Sun System: Student Challenge

STEM Lab Challenge: Design a 3-dimensional model of the Earth-sun system. The model should demonstrate the effect of rotation on sunrise, noon, sunset, and midnight.

You Should Know
Looking at the sky from Earth, the sun, moon, planets, and stars all rise in the east and set in the west. That's because Earth spins on its axis toward the east. This rotation results in day and night on the planet's surface.

Vocabulary Review
- axis
- Earth
- moon
- rotation
- sun

Materials You May Need
- globe
- heavy textbook
- clip-on lamp with 100-watt (or equivalent) light bulb
- extension cord
- other design materials: to be determined by student research

* Caution: Do not look directly at the light bulb when it is lit.

Challenge Requirements
1. <u>Research</u>: Write a one- to two-page paper summarizing your research on the Earth-sun system. Cite your sources. Your paper may include two pictures.
2. <u>Model</u>: Label a drawing of your Earth-sun model and explain your strategy.
3. <u>Results</u>: Record, analyze, and interpret test results.
4. <u>Conclusion</u>: Summarize the lab and what actually happened. It should include the purpose, a brief description of the test procedure, and explanation of results.
5. <u>Reflection</u>: Think about your team's choices for the Earth-sun model. Then complete the "Reflection" handout.
6. <u>Evaluation</u>: Think about your behavior and performance as a team member. Then complete the "Self-Evaluation Rubric."

Steps to Follow
Work with a team to complete the steps listed below. A team will have 3 or 4 members.

Step 1: Research the Earth-sun system.
Step 2: Brainstorm ideas about how to design an Earth-sun model to meet the requirements of the lab. Think about the location of the sun as Earth rotates.
Step 3: Draw a diagram of your Earth-sun design.
Step 4: Construct the model.
Step 5: Test the design and record the results.
Step 6: Evaluate the performance of your Earth-sun model.
Step 7: Identify how to improve your design.
Step 8: Make the needed changes.
Step 9: Retest and reevaluate your improved design.
Step 10: Share the results.

The Four Seasons: Teacher Information

STEM Lab Overview

Students are challenged to design a 3-dimensional model of the Earth-sun system. The model should demonstrate the effect the tilt of Earth's axis has on the heat and light received by Earth as it revolves around the sun.

Concepts

• Earth-sun system   • Season cycle

Standards for Grades 6–8

NGSS	NCTM	ITEA	CCSS
-Space Systems	-Problem Solving -Communication -Connections -Representation	-Nature of Technology -Technology and Society -Technological World	-English Language Arts Standards: Science & Technical Subjects

Teaching Strategies

Step #1: Engage—Review concepts. Introduce the STEM lab. Discuss the challenge presented in the lab, providing students with an opportunity to connect previous knowledge to the problem they are to solve.

Step #2: Investigate—Students conduct research to gain an understanding of the major science concepts related to the topic, review possible solutions to the lab challenge, and formulate new ideas for solving the problem.

Step #3: Explore—Students apply research to design and test a model, process, or system to solve the problem presented in the challenge.

Step #4: Communicate—Students share results.

Step #5: Evaluate—Students are given an opportunity to reflect on what they have learned.

Managing the Lab

• Set a deadline for project submission and presentations.
• Group students into collaborative teams and assign roles.
• Review prerequisite skills students need for doing the lab, such as measuring, weighing, constructing, recording data, graphing, and so on.
• Review science safety rules.
• Review lab cleanup procedures.
• Have the needed materials available, organized, and set up for easy access.
• Monitor teams and provide productive feedback.
• Leave enough time at the end of class for cleanup and debriefing.
• Designate area for project storage.

Evaluation

Student Reflection: Students think about their team's choices for the design of the prototype. Students individually complete the "Reflection" handout.

Student Self-Evaluation: Students think about their behavior and performance as a team member. Students individually complete the "Self-Evaluation Rubric."

Lab Evaluation: The teacher completes the "Lab Challenge Rubric" for each team.

Conference: Teacher/student conferences are held to discuss the completed evaluations.

Astronomy

The Four Seasons: Student Challenge

STEM Lab Challenge: Design a 3-dimensional model of the Earth-sun system. The model should demonstrate the effect the tilt of Earth's axis has on the heat and light received by Earth as it revolves around the sun.

You Should Know

We owe our seasons (spring, summer, fall, and winter) to the revolution of Earth around the sun and to the 23.5-degree tilt of Earth's axis.

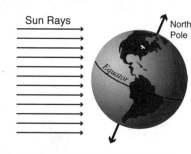

Vocabulary Review

- axis
- Earth
- revolution
- seasons
- sun

Materials You May Need

- design materials: to be determined by student research

Challenge Requirements

1. <u>Research</u>: Write a one- to two-page paper summarizing your research on the Earth-sun system and the season cycle. Cite your sources. Your paper may include two pictures.
2. <u>Model</u>: Label a drawing of your Earth-sun model. Explain your strategy.
3. <u>Results</u>: Record, analyze, and interpret test results.
4. <u>Conclusion</u>: Summarize the lab and what actually happened. It should include the purpose, a brief description of the test procedure, and explanation of results.
5. <u>Reflection</u>: Think about your team's choices for the Earth-sun model. Then complete the "Reflection" handout.
6. <u>Evaluation</u>: Think about your behavior and performance as a team member. Then complete the "Self-Evaluation Rubric."

Steps to Follow

Work with a team to complete the steps listed below. A team will have 3 or 4 members.

Step 1: Research the Earth-sun system and the season cycle.
Step 2: Brainstorm ideas about how you might design an Earth-sun model to meet the requirements of the lab. Think about how to tilt the Earth model to simulate the seasons as it revolves around the sun.
Step 3: Draw a diagram of your Earth-sun design.
Step 4: Construct the model.
Step 5: Test the design and record the results.
Step 6: Evaluate the performance of your Earth-sun model.
Step 7: Identify how to improve your design.
Step 8: Make the needed changes.
Step 9: Retest and reevaluate your improved design.
Step 10: Share the results.

Earth-Moon-Sun System: Teacher Information

STEM Lab Overview

Students are challenged to design a 3-dimensional model of the Earth-moon-sun system to demonstrate how the phases of the moon occur.

Concepts

- Earth-moon-sun system
- Phases of the moon

Standards for Grades 6–8

NGSS	NCTM	ITEA	CCSS
-Space Systems	-Problem Solving -Communication -Connections -Representation	-Nature of Technology -Technology and Society -Technological World	-English Language Arts Standards: Science & Technical Subjects

Teaching Strategies

Step #1: Engage—Review concepts. Introduce the STEM lab. Discuss the challenge presented in the lab, providing students with an opportunity to connect previous knowledge to the problem they are to solve.

Step #2: Investigate—Students conduct research to gain an understanding of the major science concepts related to the topic, review possible solutions to the lab challenge, and formulate new ideas for solving the problem.

Step #3: Explore—Students apply research to design and test a model, process, or system to solve the problem presented in the challenge.

Step #4: Communicate—Students share results.

Step #5: Evaluate—Students are given an opportunity to reflect on what they have learned.

Managing the Lab

- Set a deadline for project submission and presentations.
- Group students into collaborative teams and assign roles.
- Review prerequisite skills students need for doing the lab, such as measuring, weighing, constructing, recording data, graphing, and so on.
- Review science safety rules.
- Review lab cleanup procedures.
- Have the needed materials available, organized, and set up for easy access.
- Monitor teams and provide productive feedback.
- Leave enough time at the end of class for cleanup and debriefing.
- Designate area for project storage.

Evaluation

Student Reflection: Students think about their team's choices for the design of the prototype. Students individually complete the "Reflection" handout.

Student Self-Evaluation: Students think about their behavior and performance as a team member. Students individually complete the "Self-Evaluation Rubric."

Lab Evaluation: The teacher completes the "Lab Challenge Rubric" for each team.

Conference: Teacher/student conferences are held to discuss the completed evaluations.

Earth-Moon-Sun System: Student Challenge

STEM Lab Challenge: Design a 3-dimensional model of the Earth-moon-sun system to demonstrate how the phases of the moon occur.

You Should Know

Phases of the moon as seen in the Northern Hemisphere

| New | Waxing Crescent | 1st Qtr | Waxing Gibbous | Full | Waning Crescent | Last Qtr | Waning Gibbous |

Vocabulary Review

- Earth
- moon
- phases of the moon
- revolution
- sun

Materials You May Need

- floor lamp with 150-watt (or equivalent) bulb
- pencils
- several different sizes of Styrofoam balls
- other design materials: to be determined by student research
* Caution: Do not look directly at the light bulb when it is lit.

Challenge Requirements

1. <u>Research</u>: Write a one- to two-page paper summarizing your research on the Earth-moon-sun system and phases of the moon. Cite your sources. Your paper may include two pictures.
2. <u>Model</u>: Label a drawing of your Earth-moon-sun model and explain your strategy.
3. <u>Results</u>: Record, analyze, and interpret test results.
4. <u>Conclusion</u>: Summarize the lab and what actually happened. It should include the purpose, a brief description of the test procedure, and explanation of results.
5. <u>Reflection</u>: Think about your team's choices for the Earth-moon-sun model. Then complete the "Reflection" handout.
6. <u>Evaluation</u>: Think about your behavior and performance as a team member. Then complete the "Self-Evaluation Rubric."

Steps to Follow

Work with a team to complete the steps listed below. A team will have 3 or 4 members.

Step 1: Research the Earth-moon-sun system and phases of the moon.
Step 2: Brainstorm ideas about how you might design an Earth-moon-sun model. Think about how you can use the model to demonstrate the phases of the moon.
Step 3: Draw a diagram of your Earth-moon-sun design.
Step 4: Construct the model.
Step 5: Test the design and record the results.
Step 6: Evaluate the performance of your Earth-moon-sun model.
Step 7: Identify how to improve your design.
Step 8: Make the needed changes.
Step 9: Retest and reevaluate your improved design.
Step 10: Share the results.

Solar and Lunar Eclipses: Teacher Information

STEM Lab Overview
Students are challenged to design a 3-dimensional model of the Earth-moon-sun system and use it to demonstrate what happens during both a lunar and solar eclipse.

Concepts
• Earth-moon-sun system   • Lunar and solar eclipses

Standards for Grades 6–8

NGSS	NCTM	ITEA	CCSS
-Space Systems	-Problem Solving -Communication -Connections -Representation	-Nature of Technology -Technology and Society -Technological World	-English Language Arts Standards: Science & Technical Subjects

Teaching Strategies

Step #1: Engage—Review concepts. Introduce the STEM lab. Discuss the challenge presented in the lab, providing students with an opportunity to connect previous knowledge to the problem they are to solve.

Step #2: Investigate—Students conduct research to gain an understanding of the major science concepts related to the topic, review possible solutions to the lab challenge, and formulate new ideas for solving the problem.

Step #3: Explore—Students apply research to design and test a model, process, or system to solve the problem presented in the challenge.

Step #4: Communicate—Students share results.

Step #5: Evaluate—Students are given an opportunity to reflect on what they have learned.

Managing the Lab

• Set a deadline for project submission and presentations.
• Group students into collaborative teams and assign roles.
• Review prerequisite skills students need for doing the lab, such as measuring, weighing, constructing, recording data, graphing, and so on.
• Review science safety rules.
• Review lab cleanup procedures.
• Have the needed materials available, organized, and set up for easy access.
• Monitor teams and provide productive feedback.
• Leave enough time at the end of class for cleanup and debriefing.
• Designate area for project storage.

Evaluation

Student Reflection: Students think about their team's choices for the design of the prototype. Students individually complete the "Reflection" handout.

Student Self-Evaluation: Students think about their behavior and performance as a team member. Students individually complete the "Self-Evaluation Rubric."

Lab Evaluation: The teacher completes the "Lab Challenge Rubric" for each team.

Conference: Teacher/student conferences are held to discuss the completed evaluations.

Solar and Lunar Eclipses: Student Challenge

STEM Lab Challenge: Design a 3-dimensional model of the Earth-moon-sun system and use it to demonstrate what happens during both a lunar and solar eclipse.

You Should Know

An eclipse in space occurs when one celestial body casts a shadow on another.

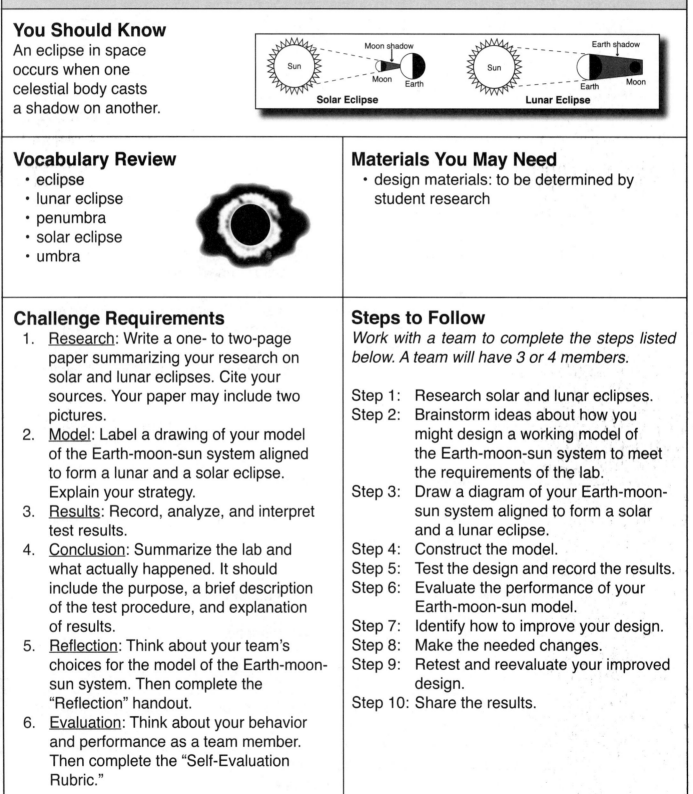

Moon shadow

Sun

Moon

Earth

Solar Eclipse

Earth shadow

Sun

Earth

Moon

Lunar Eclipse

Vocabulary Review

- eclipse
- lunar eclipse
- penumbra
- solar eclipse
- umbra

Materials You May Need

- design materials: to be determined by student research

Challenge Requirements

1. <u>Research</u>: Write a one- to two-page paper summarizing your research on solar and lunar eclipses. Cite your sources. Your paper may include two pictures.
2. <u>Model</u>: Label a drawing of your model of the Earth-moon-sun system aligned to form a lunar and a solar eclipse. Explain your strategy.
3. <u>Results</u>: Record, analyze, and interpret test results.
4. <u>Conclusion</u>: Summarize the lab and what actually happened. It should include the purpose, a brief description of the test procedure, and explanation of results.
5. <u>Reflection</u>: Think about your team's choices for the model of the Earth-moon-sun system. Then complete the "Reflection" handout.
6. <u>Evaluation</u>: Think about your behavior and performance as a team member. Then complete the "Self-Evaluation Rubric."

Steps to Follow

Work with a team to complete the steps listed below. A team will have 3 or 4 members.

Step 1:   Research solar and lunar eclipses.
Step 2:   Brainstorm ideas about how you might design a working model of the Earth-moon-sun system to meet the requirements of the lab.
Step 3:   Draw a diagram of your Earth-moon-sun system aligned to form a solar and a lunar eclipse.
Step 4:   Construct the model.
Step 5:   Test the design and record the results.
Step 6:   Evaluate the performance of your Earth-moon-sun model.
Step 7:   Identify how to improve your design.
Step 8:   Make the needed changes.
Step 9:   Retest and reevaluate your improved design.
Step 10: Share the results.

Astronomy

Moon Rover: Teacher Information

STEM Lab Overview

Students are challenged to design a rubber-band-powered moon rover that will travel a distance of two meters.

Concepts

- Moon
- Moon rover
- Newton's Laws of Motion

Standards for Grades 6–8

NGSS	NCTM	ITEA	CCSS
-Space Systems	-Problem Solving -Communication -Connections -Representation	-Nature of Technology -Technology and Society -Technological World	-English Language Arts Standards: Science & Technical Subjects

Teaching Strategies

Step #1: Engage—Review concepts. Introduce the STEM lab. Discuss the challenge presented in the lab, providing students with an opportunity to connect previous knowledge to the problem they are to solve.

Step #2: Investigate—Students conduct research to gain an understanding of the major science concepts related to the topic, review possible solutions to the lab challenge, and formulate new ideas for solving the problem.

Step #3: Explore—Students apply research to design and test a model, process, or system to solve the problem presented in the challenge.

Step #4: Communicate—Students share results.

Step #5: Evaluate—Students are given an opportunity to reflect on what they have learned.

Managing the Lab

- Set a deadline for project submission and presentations.
- Group students into collaborative teams and assign roles.
- Review prerequisite skills students need for doing the lab, such as measuring, weighing, constructing, recording data, graphing, and so on.
- Review science safety rules.
- Review lab cleanup procedures.
- Have the needed materials available, organized, and set up for easy access.
- Monitor teams and provide productive feedback.
- Leave enough time at the end of class for cleanup and debriefing.
- Designate area for project storage.

Evaluation

Student Reflection: Students think about their team's choices for the design of the prototype. Students individually complete the "Reflection" handout.

Student Self-Evaluation: Students think about their behavior and performance as a team member. Students individually complete the "Self-Evaluation Rubric."

Lab Evaluation: The teacher completes the "Lab Challenge Rubric" for each team.

Conference: Teacher/student conferences are held to discuss the completed evaluations.

Moon Rover: Student Challenge

STEM Lab Challenge: Design a rubber-band-powered moon rover that will travel a distance of two meters.

You Should Know
Moon rovers are designed to explore the surface of the moon and transmit geographical data and images back to scientists on Earth.

Vocabulary Review
- energy transfer
- friction
- kinetic energy
- potential energy
- Newton's Laws of Motion
- wheel and axle
- wheel bearings

Materials You May Need
- rubber bands
- corrugated cardboard
- scissors
- tape
- round pencils
- drinking straws
- other design materials: to be determined by student research

Challenge Requirements
1. <u>Research</u>: Write a one- to two-page paper summarizing your research on the moon, moon rovers, and Newton's Laws of Motion. Cite your sources. Your paper may include two pictures.
2. <u>Model</u>: Label a drawing of your moon rover model and explain your strategy.
3. <u>Results</u>: Record, analyze, and interpret test results.
4. <u>Conclusion</u>: Summarize the lab and what actually happened. It should include the purpose, a brief description of the test procedure, and explanation of results.
5. <u>Reflection</u>: Think about your team's choices for the moon rover model. Then complete the "Reflection" handout.
6. <u>Evaluation</u>: Think about your behavior and performance as a team member. Then complete the "Self-Evaluation Rubric."

Steps to Follow
Work with a team to complete the steps listed below. A team will have 3 or 4 members.

Step 1: Research the moon, moon rovers, and Newton's laws of motion.
Step 2: Brainstorm ideas about how to design a moon rover to meet the requirements of the lab. Think about the wheel design for your model.
Step 3: Draw a diagram of your moon rover design.
Step 4: Construct the model.
Step 5: Test the design and record the results.
Step 6: Evaluate the performance of your moon rover model.
Step 7: Identify how to improve your design.
Step 8: Make the needed changes.
Step 9: Retest and reevaluate your improved design.
Step 10: Share the results.

Lunar Lander: Teacher Information

STEM Lab Overview

Students are challenged to design a lunar lander that protects two astronauts during touchdown. When the shock-absorbing lander is dropped from a height of 30 cm, the two astronauts (regular-sized marshmallows) should not bounce out of the open cabin.

Concepts

- Gravity
- Lunar lander
- Moon

Standards for Grades 6–8

NGSS	NCTM	ITEA	CCSS
-Space Systems	-Problem Solving -Communication -Connections -Representation	-Nature of Technology -Technology and Society -Technological World	-English Language Arts Standards: Science & Technical Subjects

Teaching Strategies

Step #1: Engage—Review concepts. Introduce the STEM lab. Discuss the challenge presented in the lab, providing students with an opportunity to connect previous knowledge to the problem they are to solve.

Step #2: Investigate—Students conduct research to gain an understanding of the major science concepts related to the topic, review possible solutions to the lab challenge, and formulate new ideas for solving the problem.

Step #3: Explore—Students apply research to design and test a model, process, or system to solve the problem presented in the challenge.

Step #4: Communicate—Students share results.

Step #5: Evaluate—Students are given an opportunity to reflect on what they have learned.

Managing the Lab

- Set a deadline for project submission and presentations.
- Group students into collaborative teams and assign roles.
- Review prerequisite skills students need for doing the lab, such as measuring, weighing, constructing, recording data, graphing, and so on.
- Review science safety rules.
- Review lab cleanup procedures.
- Have the needed materials available, organized, and set up for easy access.
- Monitor teams and provide productive feedback.
- Leave enough time at the end of class for cleanup and debriefing.
- Designate area for project storage.

Evaluation

Student Reflection: Students think about their team's choices for the design of the prototype. Students individually complete the "Reflection" handout.

Student Self-Evaluation: Students think about their behavior and performance as a team member. Students individually complete the "Self-Evaluation Rubric."

Lab Evaluation: The teacher completes the "Lab Challenge Rubric" for each team.

Conference: Teacher/student conferences are held to discuss the completed evaluations.

Lunar Lander: Student Challenge

STEM Lab Challenge: Design a lunar lander that protects two astronauts during touchdown. When the shock-absorbing lander is dropped from a height of 30 cm, the two astronauts (regular-sized marshmallows) should not bounce out of the open cabin.

You Should Know
On July 20, 1969, the *Apollo 11* Lunar Module touched down in the Sea of Tranquility. The module carried two astronauts, Neil Armstrong and Edwin "Buzz" Aldrin.

Vocabulary Review
- astronaut
- gravity
- lunar lander
- moon
- shock absorber

Materials You May Need
- 1 (4 in. x 5 in.) piece of cardboard (platform)
- 1 small paper cup
- 4 (3 in. x 5 in.) index cards
- regular-sized marshmallows
- 12 miniature marshmallows
- plastic straws
- rubber bands
- scissors
- tape

Challenge Requirements
1. <u>Research</u>: Write a one- to two-page paper summarizing your research on the moon and the lunar lander. Cite your sources. Your paper may include two pictures.
2. <u>Model</u>: Label a drawing of your lunar lander model. Explain your strategy.
3. <u>Results</u>: Record, analyze, and interpret test results.
4. <u>Conclusion</u>: Summarize the lab and what actually happened. It should include the purpose, a brief description of the test procedure, and explanation of results.
5. <u>Reflection</u>: Think about your team's choices for the lunar lander model. Then complete the "Reflection" handout.
6. <u>Evaluation</u>: Think about your behavior and performance as a team member. Then complete the "Self-Evaluation Rubric."

Steps to Follow
Work with a team to complete the steps listed below. A team will have 3 or 4 members.

Step 1: Research the moon and the lunar lander.

Step 2: Brainstorm ideas about how you might design a lunar lander to meet the requirements of the lab. Think about weight distribution, the placement of the astronaut cabin, and shock absorbers.

Step 3: Draw a diagram of your lunar lander design.

Step 4: Construct the model.

Step 5: Test the design and record the results (make sure the lander is level when releasing for landing).

Step 6: Evaluate the performance of your lunar lander model.

Step 7: Identify how to improve your design.

Step 8: Make the needed changes.

Step 9: Retest and reevaluate your improved design.

Step 10: Share the results.

Sunspots: Teacher Information

STEM Lab Overview
Students are challenged to design a process for tracking the movement of sunspots.

Concepts
• Sun • Sun-viewing safety rules • Telescope

Standards for Grades 6–8			
NGSS	**NCTM**	**ITEA**	**CCSS**
-Space Systems	-Problem Solving -Communication -Connections -Representation	-Nature of Technology -Technology and Society -Technological World	-English Language Arts Standards: Science & Technical Subjects

Teaching Strategies

Step #1: Engage—Review concepts. Introduce the STEM lab. Discuss the challenge presented in the lab, providing students with an opportunity to connect previous knowledge to the problem they are to solve.

Step #2: Investigate—Students conduct research to gain an understanding of the major science concepts related to the topic, review possible solutions to the lab challenge, and formulate new ideas for solving the problem.

Step #3: Explore—Students apply research to design and test a model, process, or system to solve the problem presented in the challenge.

Step #4: Communicate—Students share results.

Step #5: Evaluate—Students are given an opportunity to reflect on what they have learned.

Managing the Lab

- Set a deadline for project submission and presentations.
- Group students into collaborative teams and assign roles.
- Review prerequisite skills students need for doing the lab, such as measuring, weighing, constructing, recording data, graphing, and so on.
- Review science safety rules.
- Review lab cleanup procedures.
- Have the needed materials available, organized, and set up for easy access.
- Monitor teams and provide productive feedback.
- Leave enough time at the end of class for cleanup and debriefing.
- Designate area for project storage.

Evaluation

Student Reflection: Students think about their team's choices for the design of the prototype. Students individually complete the "Reflection" handout.

Student Self-Evaluation: Students think about their behavior and performance as a team member. Students individually complete the "Self-Evaluation Rubric."

Lab Evaluation: The teacher completes the "Lab Challenge Rubric" for each team.

Conference: Teacher/student conferences are held to discuss the completed evaluations.

Astronomy

Sunspots: Student Challenge

STEM Lab Challenge: Design a process for tracking the movement of sunspots.

You Should Know
Sun Safety Rules:
- Do not look directly at the sun with the naked eye.
- Do not view the sun directly with any unfiltered optical device, such as binoculars or a telescope.

Vocabulary Review
- rotation
- sun
- sunspots
- telescope

Materials You May Need
- cardboard with hole cut in center
- small tripod
- small refracting telescope
- other design materials: to be determined by student research

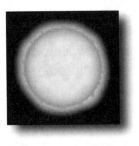

Challenge Requirements
1. <u>Research</u>: Write a one- to two-page paper summarizing your research on the sun and sunspots. Cite your sources. Your paper may include two pictures.
2. <u>Model</u>: Label a drawing of your process and explain your strategy.
3. <u>Results</u>: Record, analyze, and interpret test results.
4. <u>Conclusion</u>: Summarize the lab and what actually happened. It should include the purpose, a brief description of the test procedure, and explanation of results.
5. <u>Reflection</u>: Think about your team's choices for the tracking process. Then complete the "Reflection" handout.
6. <u>Evaluation</u>: Think about your behavior and performance as a team member. Then complete the "Self-Evaluation Rubric."

Steps to Follow
Work with a team to complete the steps listed below. A team will have 3 or 4 members.

Step 1: Research the sun and sunspots.
Step 2: Brainstorm ideas about how you might design a process for tracking the movement of sunspots to meet the requirements of the lab.
Step 3: Draw a diagram of your tracking process.
Step 4: Set up the process.
Step 5: Test the process and record the results.
Step 6: Evaluate the performance of your tracking process.
Step 7: Identify how to improve your process.
Step 8: Make the needed changes.
Step 9: Retest and reevaluate your improved process.
Step 10: Share the results.

Astronomy

Make a Telescope: Teacher Information

STEM Lab Overview

Students are challenged to design a telescope to view stars and planets in the night sky.

Concepts

• Refracting telescopes   • Reflecting telescopes

Standards for Grades 6–8

NGSS	NCTM	ITEA	CCSS
-Space Systems	-Problem Solving -Communication -Connections -Representation	-Nature of Technology -Technology and Society -Technological World	-English Language Arts Standards: Science & Technical Subjects

Teaching Strategies

Step #1: Engage—Review concepts. Introduce the STEM lab. Discuss the challenge presented in the lab, providing students with an opportunity to connect previous knowledge to the problem they are to solve.

Step #2: Investigate—Students conduct research to gain an understanding of the major science concepts related to the topic, review possible solutions to the lab challenge, and formulate new ideas for solving the problem.

Step #3: Explore—Students apply research to design and test a model, process, or system to solve the problem presented in the challenge.

Step #4: Communicate—Students share results.

Step #5: Evaluate—Students are given an opportunity to reflect on what they have learned.

Managing the Lab

• Set a deadline for project submission and presentations.
• Group students into collaborative teams and assign roles.
• Review prerequisite skills students need for doing the lab, such as measuring, weighing, constructing, recording data, graphing, and so on.
• Review science safety rules.
• Review lab cleanup procedures.
• Have the needed materials available, organized, and set up for easy access.
• Monitor teams and provide productive feedback.
• Leave enough time at the end of class for cleanup and debriefing.
• Designate area for project storage.

Evaluation

Student Reflection: Students think about their team's choices for the design of the prototype. Students individually complete the "Reflection" handout.
Student Self-Evaluation: Students think about their behavior and performance as a team member. Students individually complete the "Self-Evaluation Rubric."
Lab Evaluation: The teacher completes the "Lab Challenge Rubric" for each team.
Conference: Teacher/student conferences are held to discuss the completed evaluations.

Make a Telescope: Student Challenge

STEM Lab Challenge: Design a telescope to view stars and planets in the night sky.

You Should Know
A telescope is an instrument used to see distant objects more clearly. There are two main types of telescopes. A refracting telescope uses lenses to bend light to magnify the image. A reflecting telescope uses mirrors to focus the light of the image.

Vocabulary Review
- aperture
- concave mirror
- convex lens
- focal point
- lens
- light
- magnification
- mirrors
- reflecting
- refracting

Materials You May Need
- magnifying glass
- masking tape
- scissors
- flat mirror
- two paper towel tubes
- meter stick
- other design materials: to be determined by student research

* Caution: Do not view the sun directly with any unfiltered optical device, such as binoculars or a telescope.

Challenge Requirements
1. <u>Research</u>: Write a one- to two-page paper summarizing your research on refracting and reflecting telescopes. Cite your sources. Your paper may include two pictures.
2. <u>Model</u>: Label a drawing of your telescope and explain your strategy.
3. <u>Results</u>: Record, analyze, and interpret test results.
4. <u>Conclusion</u>: Summarize the lab and what actually happened. It should include the purpose, a brief description of the test procedure, and explanation of results.
5. <u>Reflection</u>: Think about your team's choices for the telescope. Then complete the "Reflection" handout.
6. <u>Evaluation</u>: Think about your behavior and performance as a team member. Then complete the "Self-Evaluation Rubric."

Steps to Follow
Work with a team to complete the steps listed below. A team will have 3 or 4 members.

Step 1: Research refracting and reflecting telescopes.
Step 2: Brainstorm ideas about how to design a telescope model to meet the requirements of the lab. Think about which telescope you will design.
Step 3: Draw a diagram of your telescope design.
Step 4: Construct the model.
Step 5: Test the design and record the results.
Step 6: Evaluate the performance of your telescope model.
Step 7: Identify how to improve your design.
Step 8: Make the needed changes.
Step 9: Retest and reevaluate your improved design.
Step 10: Share the results.

Inflatable Planetarium: Teacher Information

STEM Lab Overview

Students are challenged to design a life-size inflatable planetarium. The planetarium should display the major constellations visible in the northern hemisphere during the winter season. Several students at a time should be able to sit in the planetarium and view the simulated night sky.

Concepts

• Constellations
• Planetarium
• Stars

Standards for Grades 6–8

NGSS	NCTM	ITEA	CCSS
-Space Systems	-Problem Solving -Communication -Connections -Representation	-Nature of Technology -Technology and Society -Technological World	-English Language Arts Standards: Science & Technical Subjects

Teaching Strategies

Step #1: Engage—Review concepts. Introduce the STEM lab. Discuss the challenge presented in the lab, providing students with an opportunity to connect previous knowledge to the problem they are to solve.

Step #2: Investigate—Students conduct research to gain an understanding of the major science concepts related to the topic, review possible solutions to the lab challenge, and formulate new ideas for solving the problem.

Step #3: Explore—Students apply research to design and test a model, process, or system to solve the problem presented in the challenge.

Step #4: Communicate—Students share results.

Step #5: Evaluate—Students are given an opportunity to reflect on what they have learned.

Managing the Lab

• Set a deadline for project submission and presentations.
• Group students into collaborative teams and assign roles.
• Review prerequisite skills students need for doing the lab, such as measuring, weighing, constructing, recording data, graphing, and so on.
• Review science safety rules.
• Review lab cleanup procedures.
• Have the needed materials available, organized, and set up for easy access.
• Monitor teams and provide productive feedback.
• Leave enough time at the end of class for cleanup and debriefing.
• Designate area for project storage.

Evaluation

Student Reflection: Students think about their team's choices for the design of the prototype. Students individually complete the "Reflection" handout.

Student Self-Evaluation: Students think about their behavior and performance as a team member. Students individually complete the "Self-Evaluation Rubric."

Lab Evaluation: The teacher completes the "Lab Challenge Rubric" for each team.

Conference: Teacher/student conferences are held to discuss the completed evaluations.

Astronomy

Inflatable Planetarium: **Student Challenge**

STEM Lab Challenge: Design a life-size inflatable planetarium. The planetarium should display the major constellations visible in the northern hemisphere during the winter season. Several students at a time should be able to sit in the planetarium and view the simulated night sky.

You Should Know
Astronomers officially recognize a total of 88 constellations. Different constellations are visible at different times of the year. Constellations seen in the southern hemisphere are different from those seen in the northern hemisphere.

Vocabulary Review
- constellation
- planetarium
- stars

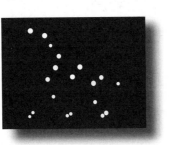

Materials You May Need
- box fan
- 20 ft. x 50 ft. black plastic sheeting
- utility tape
- scissors
- other design materials: to be determined by student research

Challenge Requirements
1. <u>Research</u>: Write a one- to two-page paper summarizing your research on stars and constellations. Cite your sources. Your paper may include two pictures.
2. <u>Model</u>: Label a drawing of your inflatable planetarium. Explain your strategy.
3. <u>Results</u>: Record, analyze, and interpret test results.
4. <u>Conclusion</u>: Summarize the lab and what actually happened. It should include the purpose, a brief description of the test procedure, and explanation of results.
5. <u>Reflection</u>: Think about your team's choices for the inflatable planetarium. Then complete the "Reflection" handout.
6. <u>Evaluation</u>: Think about your behavior and performance as a team member. Then complete the "Self-Evaluation Rubric."

Steps to Follow
Work with a team to complete the steps listed below. A team will have 3 or 4 members.

Step 1: Research stars and constellations.
Step 2: Brainstorm ideas about how you might design a life-size inflatable model of a planetarium to meet the requirements of the lab.
Step 3: Draw a diagram of your planetarium design.
Step 4: Construct the model.
Step 5: Test the design of the planetarium. Test the accuracy of the formation of the constellations using your science book or other resources. Record the results.
Step 6: Evaluate the performance of your planetarium model.
Step 7: Identify how to improve your design.
Step 8: Make the needed changes.
Step 9: Retest and reevaluate your improved design.
Step 10: Share the results.